HENRY KIRKE WHITE

By RICHARD D. MCGHEE

Kansas State University

TWAYNE PUBLISHERS

A DIVISION OF G. K. HALL & CO., BOSTON

Copyright © 1981 by G. K. Hall & Co.

Published in 1981 by Twayne Publishers,
A Division of G. K. Hall & Co.
All Rights Reserved

Printed on permanent/durable acid-free paper and bound
in the United States of America

First Printing

Library of Congress Cataloging in Publication Data

McGhee, Richard D. 1940 -
Henry Kirke White.

(Twayne's English authors series; TEAS 318)
Bibliography: p. **166**
Includes index.
1. White, Henry Kirke, 1785 - 1806—Criticism and
interpretation.
PR5794.M3   821'.7   80-19116
ISBN 0-8057-6808-4

TWAYNE'S ENGLISH AUTHORS SERIES

DATE DUE

DEMCO 38-297

TEAS 318

Engraving of Henry Kirke White by H. Robinson.
Reprinted by permission of Bell & Hyman Publishers.

To
my daughter,
Beth

Contents

About the Author
Preface
Acknowledgments
Chronology

1. Life, Character, and Literary Taste 15
2. *Melancholy Hours:* Solitary Effusions to the Public 33
3. In the Picturesque Tradition: Poetry for the Eye 54
4. In the Tradition of the Beautiful: Poetry for the Ear 77
5. In the Tradition of the Sublime: Poetry for the Mind 114

Notes and References 159
Selected Bibliography 166
Index 171

About the Author

Richard D. McGhee was born in Rogers County, Oklahoma. He attended high school in Kansas City, Missouri, and earned his B.A. at the University of Missouri at Kansas City. He then attended the University of Oklahoma, where he earned his M.A. and Ph.D. in English and American Literature. He has published essays on Burke, Wordsworth, Tennyson, Browning, Clough, Swinburne, and Whitman. His book *Marriage, Duty and Desire in Victorian Poetry and Drama* was published by the Regents Press of Kansas in 1980. Richard McGhee is currently professor of English and head of the Department at Kansas State University.

Preface

When Robert Southey and Lord Byron could agree upon something important to them both, we are naturally curious. This study of Henry Kirke White's poetry is an attempt to satisfy such a curiosity. For Southey and Byron agreed that this young man's life and poetry were deserving of the public's attention, and even admiration. Shortly after White's death in 1806, Southey published *The Life and Remains of Henry Kirke White;* Southey wished "to lay before the world some account of one whose early death is not less to be lamented as a loss to English literature, and whose virtues were as admirable as his genius."[1] About the same time, Byron lamented "Unhappy White!" in "English Bards and Scotch Reviewers":[2]

> Unhappy White! while life was in its spring,
> And thy young muse just waved her joyous wing,
> The spoiler swept that soaring lyre away,
> Which else had sounded an immortal lay. (831 - 34)

Both Southey and Byron saw more promise than accomplishment in Kirke White's poetry, but they both defended the quality of what had been done, nevertheless. As late as 1811 we find Byron defending White's poetry against the criticism of R. C. Dallas:

I am sorry you don't like Harry White, with a great deal Of Cant which in him was sincere . . . certes there is Poesy & Genius, (I don't say this on account of my Simile & rhymes) but surely he was beyond all the Bloomfields & Blacketts & their collateral coblers. . . .[3]

Six days later Byron again writes Dallas, insisting on "Harry White's Genius" so much that "he surely ranks next Chatterton."[4] The vigor of Byron's defense and the sincerity of Southey's praise require more than passing interest.

Kirke White did not live long enough to write much, and while he was alive he did not have much time to give to his writing. But since he began writing as early as fourteen, he had as many as seven years of "creative" activity. Indeed, even had he lived longer, those seven years may have been all he would have given to poetry (for there are signs he might have abandoned it upon entering the ministry). He had, therefore, a small but respectable body of poetry to give the world, approximately 100 poems in various stages of completion. Most are short poems, but some are as long as 500 to 600 lines. In addition, White wrote several prose essays, many of which were published in his lifetime.

I have not attempted to examine all of his writing, even in a long study of a short canon. I have not said much about his very few love lyrics or about his poems of social protest (such as "The Wonderful Juggler" and "The Prostitute"), for my main interest has been to examine the ways his poetry strives for an authentic voice, even struggles with the various poetic traditions and aesthetic trends that lay behind him. I have chosen three terms critical for any study of the era: the picturesque, the beautiful, and the sublime. These are not arbitrary, although sometimes my choice of poems for discussion under the rubric of one of these terms may seem arbitrary to some readers. In my discussion, I attempt to show how White's poetry benefited and suffered from his conscious adaptation or even imitation of works that established these traditions.

One danger, of which I have tried to be constantly aware, is to become so involved in the analysis of one of the poems by this admittedly immature poet, that all sense of proportion is lost. I realize that some of my discussion will sound as if I believe his poetry is great, merely because I am giving so much attention to it. But Kirke White's poetry is only sometimes good, never great. He wrote some fine things, regardless of his age, but for the most part he was still learning how to write when suddenly he died at the deplorably early age of twenty-one.

RICHARD D. MCGHEE

Kansas State University

Acknowledgments

I wish to acknowledge the support of the following in the making of this book: the Bureau of General Research, and Robert F. Kruh, dean of the Graduate School, Kansas State University; William L. Stamey, dean of the College of Arts and Sciences, Kansas State University, whose support of a sabbatical leave from administrative and teaching responsibilities has given me the time to complete this project; Karen K. Caffrey, for her patience and skill in typing the manuscript; and my daughter, Beth, whose love has been a continuing inspiration.

Chronology

1785 Henry Kirke White born in Nottingham, March 21. Second son of John and Mary White.
1791 Placed under the instruction of Rev. John Blanchard, Nottingham.
1797 Removed to instruction of a Mr. Shipley, Nottingham.
1798 Composes his first poem (to be preserved). His mother opens a Ladies' Boarding and Day School in Nottingham.
1799 Removed from school and placed in a stocking-loom. Later placed in the office of Messrs. Coldham and Enfield, town clerks and attorneys of Nottingham, sometime in May. Begins correspondence with his brother Neville, a medical student in London, in September. Begins study of Latin, Greek, Italian, Spanish, and Portuguese, while reading law. Elected "Professor of Literature" by members of a Nottingham Literary Society after hearing his lecture on "Genius."
1800 Wins a silver medal for a translation from Horace, published (?) in the *Monthly Preceptor*, c. June. Begins to experience religious doubts.
1801 Wins a pair of globes for an imaginary tour from London to Edinburgh, published in the *Monthly Preceptor*, c. April. Has an essay on "Gratitude" published in the *Monthly Preceptor*, April, and an essay on "Truth" published in the *Monthly Visitor*, also in April. Becomes a regular contributor to the *Monthly Mirror* with the publication of an essay on Thomas Warton, the Younger. His writing attracts the notice of Capel Lofft (patron of Robert Bloomfield) and Thomas Hill, proprietor of the *Monthly Mirror*.
1802 Lofft and Hill encourage him to prepare a volume of his poems for publication. Articled to study law with Coldham and Enfield.
1803 After being refused by the Countess of Derby, he secures

the permission of the Duchess of Devonshire to dedicate his poems to her. Publishes *Clifton Grove, a Sketch in Verse, with other Poems,* a small 12 mo. volume of 126 pages. Coldham and Enfield offered to cancel his articles so that he might attend the university to prepare for the ministry. Friends attempt to arrange for financial assistance.

1804 Hostile review of his book in the *Monthly Review,* February. His letter of reply seen by Southey, who writes to encourage and commend his work. Decides, in June, to study for the ministry. But learns, in July, that his plans for attending Trinity College, Cambridge, have collapsed. Returns to his study of the law and thinks of becoming a religious dissenter. Begins to fear he has consumption. Learns that a sizarship at St. John's College, Cambridge, is available for him, and, in preparation for his matriculation, "degrades" to Winteringham, Lincolnshire, for study with a Rev. Grainger for a year, August.

1805 Admitted as a Sizar at St. John's College, October. Reads for the university scholarship, November. In London for rest, December.

1806 Learns that he achieved a "first" in his general college examinations, January. Back to Cambridge, where his health continues to suffer. Again achieves a "first" in his examinations, June. The college makes a tutor available to him for summer study. In July awarded an exhibition with an income of £63 per year. Declines the mastership of the Free-School at Nottingham, August. Visits his brother in London for a few days, and then returns to Cambridge, where he dies 19 October. Buried in the Church of All Saints, Cambridge, on the north side of the chancel. Robert Southey offers to assist in arranging publication of the complete works.

1807 *The Life and Remains,* with "An Account of the Life," by Robert Southey published.

1819 A tablet to his memory, with a medallion by Chantrey and an inscription by Prof. William Smyth, placed above his grave at the expense of a young American, Francis Boott of Boston.

1823 Tenth edition of *The Life and Remains.*

1829 First American edition of *The Life and Remains.*

CHAPTER 1

Life, Character, and Literary Taste

I *Biographical Sketch*

ROBERT Southey, in 1807, published *The Complete Works of Henry Kirke White of Nottingham, Late of St. John's College, Cambridge, with an Account of His Life.* By 1823 the book was in its tenth edition and in 1829 it was published in America, where it went through several more editions. Assisted by Southey's *Life* and Byron's tribute in "English Bards and Scotch Reviewers," Kirke White's poetry was widely read and applauded on both sides of the Atlantic. We may be perplexed to understand why this should have been so, for the poetry is more a matter of promise than real accomplishment, but we can appreciate the interest more readily if we keep in mind the youth of the poet, his difficult circumstances in life, and his deplorably early death.

Henry Kirke White was born 21 March 1785, the second son of John and Mary White. His father was a butcher in the city of Nottingham, and his mother, born Neville, was to open a boarding school for young women when Kirke was thirteen. The trade of the father and the business of the mother suggest the conflicting pressures which Kirke would experience throughout his young life, for his father wanted his sons quickly to learn trades that would earn them livings and his mother apparently desired for them something more ambitious. The older son, Neville, went to London to study medicine (which he gave up to enter the ministry in 1829) and there he was during Kirke's university career; Neville was to be Kirke's confidant and generous supporter. Kirke himself was placed to work at the age of thirteen in a Nottingham stocking loom. Since this occurred at the same time his mother opened the boarding school, there may have been an economic crisis in the family fortunes.

The boy did not stay long at the loom, for he was placed in the law office of Messrs. Coldham and Enfield in May 1799, only a few months after beginning work at the stocking loom. This was to be the real beginning of his better fortune, for Coldham and Enfield seem to have been sympathetic masters. They accepted the boy without immediately receiving the fee for articling him and they would later forgive his bond when a more auspicious career opened up for Kirke. In his earliest surviving letter, Kirke wrote in September 1799 to his brother Neville that he liked his "business," because it was something he "chose" from several others.[1] Kirke's early letters have the stilted tone of self-conscious but intelligent adolescence, and this remark to Neville may have been an exaggeration of his independence to determine his life as well as an understandable enthusiasm for a professional opportunity.

During the first year of his law apprenticeship, Kirke began studying several languages, including Latin, Greek, and Italian. In this, as in most other intellectual endeavors, he was very successful. He later added a smattering of French, Spanish, and Portuguese, although in these he was less proficient. Besides reading law, carrying out a clerk's responsibilities in the office, and studying languages, Kirke was reading prose fiction and poetry, which he was writing as well. He had composed poetry as early as 1798, when Southey dates the earliest surviving poem, "On Being Confined to School One Pleasant Morning in Spring," and he continued to compose with rapid improvement in skill and knowledge.

In June 1800 he wrote Neville that their "mother has allowed [him] a good deal lately for books."[2] He was proud of his growing library, and he was equally proud of his economy of time and money. His favorite book, at least for current utility, was *Robinson Crusoe,* which he recommended to his brother as "the best novel for youth in the English language." Kirke probably realized that Robinson Crusoe was in his blood long before he ever read the book. Like Defoe's hero, Kirke White was having to make do with very little means and in opposition to some unsympathetic circumstances (including a father who could not afford to support the kind of education his boy desired). A constant refrain of Kirke's writings is his rationalization of his creative talent for poetry when he had little leisure for cultivating such a "useless" activity.

He explained that he read fiction to afford him some "necessary relaxation" after hours of "fatiguing researches in

Blackstone or Coke."³ He gave an account of heavy reading, from Plutarch through Smith's *Wealth of Nations* to Goldsmith's *Essays*, and he told his brother he had subscribed to the *British Classics*, a volume of which he received every fortnight. He told Neville, with some embarrassment, that he had lately "turned poet" for he translated an ode of Horace into English and submitted it for publication to the *Monthly Preceptor*. Because, however, he "forgot" to title it when he submitted it, he did not expect it to be noticed. Kirke was probably not being entirely honest, since his first attempts were circumscribed by diffidence and uncertainty and he probably hoped for publication without being identified.

Nevertheless, by the age of fourteen he discovered throughout the hardships of his apprenticeship in the law that his "chief delight" was poetry.⁴ He prided himself that he was forming his taste by reading the "best poets," those published with the *Lives* written by Samuel Johnson. Therefore Kirke White was learning from Johnson that Pope and Dryden were the best models for imitation, but he was also acquiring a taste for much poetry included in that series which Johnson might not have approved for his imitation, including Milton, Thomson, Young, Gray, and Mark Akenside. These latter proved to be very influential upon the boy's imagination, catching his taste for sentiment, melancholy, and themes of human mortality.

The subject of original genius (as opposed to imitation of the classics) which so preoccupied the two generations of English writers who preceded Henry Kirke White was also the subject on which he first made himself known to the literary community. That group was obviously much impressed when this boy of fourteen lectured them for two hours on "Genius."⁵ Those anonymous gentlemen (and ladies?) paid Kirke the great compliment of electing him their "professor of literature"! We do not know if they were serious or mocking or merely fatigued. But certainly the boy was serious, not mocking, and far from fatigued. He had not a great sense of humor, but he had much pride in himself for his achievements against much adversity. He began to lecture his elders very early in his essays and poems which he published in the *Monthly Preceptor* and, later, in the *Monthly Mirror*.

At the same time he was studying and translating Latin literature (including the ode from Horace which he mentioned to his brother and for which he won a silver medal after its publication), Kirke was beginning to experience religious doubts. He had not been much interested in religious matters before 1800, but about that time he read an evangelical tract, Scott's *Force of Truth,* and later he began to think much upon religious subjects. By August 1801 he wrote to a Mr. Booth that he had just completed reading "Jones on the Trinity"; he admits that until then "religious polemics, indeed, have seldom formed a part of [his] studies."[6] But his recent reading has saved him from trying to get to heaven on his own account, and so "the mists which [his] ignorance had conjured around" him were cleared away.[7] He became more interested in religion, including Evangelical Christianity, until he went to the university, when his religion became more orthodox at the same time it became more intense.

Kirke began regular contributions to the *Monthly Mirror* sometime in early 1801. One of his first essays was on Thomas Warton, the Younger, and his later series of *Melancholy Hours* (in twelve numbers) shows the heavy influence of such writers as Warton on Kirke's style and subject matter. These essays attracted the notice of Mr. Capel Lofft, the patron of Robert Bloomfield, and Mr. Thomas Hill, the proprietor of the *Mirror.* These two men saw literary promise in the works of the sixteen-year-old boy, and they encouraged him to prepare a volume of his poems for publication. Of course, Kirke was flattered and immediately began to put his poems together for the world. By early 1803 he had progressed sufficiently to look about for a patronness to whom he might dedicate his poems and so secure some more promise of success than a young unknown had any right to expect. His brother became Kirke's emissary to the London nobility to solicit permission for the dedication. The Countess of Derby refused to accept his dedication, but the Duchess of Devonshire did condescend after many frustrating efforts to contact her, to allow Kirke to dedicate the volume to her. The experience was a trying one for both Neville and Kirke, but they finally succeeded in their objective and saw the publication of the volume under the title of *Clifton Grove, a Sketch in Verse, with Other Poems,* a small duodecimo volume of 126 pages. It was to be the only volume of Kirke White's poetry published in his short lifetime.

Besides learning something about the condescension of the nobility toward aspiring writers of the lower classes, Kirke began immediately upon the publication of his book to learn something about the world of literary competition. Among the notices his book received was one in the *Monthly Review* for February 1804 which commended Kirke's "exertions, and his laudable endeavours to excel; but we cannot compliment him with having learned the difficult art of writing good poetry."[8] This was severe, but just, criticism. Like so much literary criticism of the day, however, it tended toward the *ad hominem* and so provoked Kirke to a reply which defended his good character and independent spirit. Both the volume of poems and the critical exchange between the reviewer and Kirke White caught the attention of the man who would do more than anyone else to establish the young poet as a promising worthy: Robert Southey.

Southey saw the letter Kirke had written to the *Monthly Review*, read the review article, sympathized with the predicament of the young author, and then read some of Kirke White's poetry. He found "strong marks of genius" in the poems, even the ones which had been criticized by the review.[9] Southey struck up a correspondence with White and joined a growing band of supporters for the young man's genius. In his gracious reply to Southey, Kirke informed him of his ambition to "produce something which will survive."[10] Southey offered his assistance for any future efforts to publish, especially should Kirke decide to publish by subscription (which Southey advised him to do). But by this time Kirke had made a radical turn in his life.

Although he would not give up his ambition to write poetry, Kirke had by 1803 grown increasingly discontent with his situation as an apprentice for the law and asked to be released from his articles with Coldham and Enfield. The reason for this change of direction was mainly one of intellectual ambition. Kirke's growing circle of friends encouraged his high estimate of his talents and abilities until he decided that he must give them a better chance through university training. His opportunity had to be made, however, for such a thing did not simply happen to someone in his family's circumstances. First, he had to decide that his career would be in the Church establishment, and that was not a difficult decision for him to make since his interest in religion was increasingly intense. He began to identify his earthly fortune, specifically his prospect for financial aid to attend the university, with God's judgment, and as his hopes rose or declined, he tended to preach to his brother about Christian doctrine or to mourn his own sinful state. Kirke White was a confused young man in 1803-1804.

He wanted to be a success in life. He wanted literary fame probably more than he wanted to write good literature. But behind that lay his hope that fame might make it possible for him to secure a livelihood which would rescue him from the drudgery of his parents' lives. The elements of good fortune began to fall into place in 1804. When financial arrangements made it possible for him finally to attend St. John's College, Cambridge (after earlier plans for Trinity fell through), Henry could definitely give up the law and do what he discovered was in his real nature: to study for the ministry of Christ. One ominous fact that entered into his plans was his discovery that he was losing his hearing. He told his brother sometime in 1803 that his "wish to enter the church" was connected with belief that his "deafness [might not be] removed."[11] Loss of hearing threatened to make Kirke ineligible for a successful law career, although it pointed him toward a life of more liberal study, the kind of life he desired for himself anyway. The Church was the place for a thoughtful, sensitive young man of Kirke White's day, and in that solid establishment deafness might even prove to be a positive virtue. On the other hand, his ailment was one of several symptoms that would gather to suggest his generally poor health. The foundation was being laid for the myth that his intellectual endeavors killed him.

After much anxiety that he would not be able to raise the funds necessary to support him at the university, Kirke learned that a sizarship to St. John's was available for him, and that, together with help from his mother and a few friends, was all he needed to be on his way. Coldham and Enfield released him from his articles, and Kirke went off for a year's study with a tutor at Winteringham, Lincolnshire, before going to Cambridge. While there he showed more signs of a deteriorating physical condition, but he nevertheless thrived upon his newly found intellectual milieu. His letters written from Winteringham between August 1804 and September 1805 are filled with gusto and excitement; they show us a real personality beginning to break through the stilted prose of affectation which plagued his earlier, childish letters. During this year of intense study he learned Greek and mathematics, read much philosophy, practiced Latin composition, and thought a good deal about the meaning of Christianity. But he also joined in various boating and hiking excursions which not only lifted his animal spirits but also kept some balance in his life between his tendency to melancholy self-examination and a genuinely sincere interest in the beauty of the natural landscape.

Although he gives hints of a continued opposition from his father, Kirke spent a successful year at Winteringham.[12] He went up to Cambridge in the fall term of 1805; and so he just missed being a college mate of Lord Byron, who had taken residence at Trinity while Kirke went to St. John's. It is possible that Byron met or heard of White during the 1805-1806 school season, but their university careers were dramatically opposite in direction. White was to be famous as a scholar while Byron was establishing his notorious reputation for sensual disdain of intellectual pursuits. The year at St. John's was a very successful and satisfying year for Kirke, since he not only achieved "firsts" in his general examinations but he also attracted the notice of those who could ensure his financial security. His first summer after entering the university saw him remain at his college to benefit from a tutor whose services were provided free by the college. Thus he had little relief from the intense regimen of study which had begun when he went to Winteringham. The atmosphere of St. John's was perhaps a little awesome and even intimidating to the young man at his first entrance. He felt he had to prove himself, and so he exerted his energy more than most of the new scholars of his day. He was proud of his accomplishments, but he was trying hard to be humble.

He had reason to be proud, but he also had increasing reason to be humble because his health was failing. He spent his vacation periods at home in Nottingham and with his brother and their aunt in London. The tutoring session for the summer kept him at his studies when he should probably have been resting for his health. However, there is little evidence to suggest that Henry Kirke White would have survived even with an extended period of rest. He suffered continuing loss of hearing, symptoms of a chronic cold, fainting spells, and maybe even an epileptic seizure.[13] After a week's visit with his brother in London in September 1806, Kirke returned to his studies at St. John's and died there, alone, on 19 October. In his pocket was an unfinished letter to his brother telling him that his illness had increased so much that he could not plan to attend the lectures which were to begin within the week. That was a telling admission for White to make.

II "A Chaos of all Contradiction": The Complexity of His Character

Southey printed in his "Life" a poem by Kirke White on "[His] Own Character."[14] The poem was "addressed (during illness) to a lady" whom he calls "Fanny" in the poem. Southey used the poem to illustrate Kirke's religious uncertainty when he was fifteen or sixteen years of age. It is difficult, however, to take full soberly the sentiments of a poem which begins by describing the speaker as "laid on the shelf" during his illness and which compares the speaker to "a penitent nun" who tells all personal faults during confession. He banters Fanny with an admonition to "put that curling brow down" when she apparently expressed some disapproval of his light-hearted treatment of nuns and priests. Nevertheless, if we are to take the poem to tell us anything about White's state of mind when he was fifteen or sixteen (as Southey says we should), we will learn from it that the boy is in "a chaos of all contradiction" between "religion" and "deism," between loyalty to the monarchy and enthusiasm for democratic reforms, and between sad moodiness and gay thoughtlessness.

Kirke White inherited a set of divided values, the fate of sensitive persons living in the second half of the eighteenth century in England. He had to overcome the increasing opposition between rationalism and Christianity, between natural science and religious faith. Somehow he had to resolve the differences in his mind and heart or he had to live "in divided and distinguished worlds," as Thomas Browne had described the "amphibious" nature of man (*Religio Medici*, 1642). Many tried to unify these divided worlds, or at least to bridge them; one group followed Browne in agreeing with him that "nature is the art of God." This group argued that revelation was not necessary to true religion, for in reason and nature there was sufficient cause for faith. In the eighteenth century this group included some illustrious men, advocating what Leslie Stephen calls "constructive deism."[15] From John Locke's *Reasonableness of Christianity* (1695), to Matthew Tindal's *Christianity as Old as the Creation* (1730), to Thomas Paine's *Age of Reason* (1795), there is a continuity of interest in maintaining the sufficiency of reason for human faith. On the other hand there was a rival tradition in what Leslie Stephen calls "critical deism."¹⁶ David Hume's essay "On Miracles" (1748) proved that miracles are impossible because they are contrary to the laws of nature, and there followed Hume a distinguished line of thinkers that included Edward Gibbon and Horace Walpole, believing that the traditional religion was irrational and absurd and that no amount of reasoning could find God in nature.

While the debates of the deists, whether constructive or critical, lingered in the background during Kirke White's lifetime, the strongest and most influential thinkers for White himself were men like Joseph Butler and William Paley, whose opposition to the deist arguments rests upon the proposition that the laws of God can best be known by analogy with the laws of nature. In his *Analogy of Religion to the Constitution and Course of Nature* (1736), Butler set out to demonstrate that the God of Revelation is the God of Nature, and he did so mainly by emphasizing the mysterious ways of God in nature—ways quite as baffling to human reason as are the mysterious ways of God in Revelation. Although, Butler says, "Christianity is a scheme as much above our comprehension, as that of nature," mankind may nevertheless learn by methods of analogy that "there is a kind of moral government implied in God's natural government [where] virtue and vice are naturally rewarded and punished as beneficial and mischievous to society."¹⁷ With his emphasis on the dark and mysterious features of nature as consistent with the God of religion, Butler's argument had a great appeal to Kirke White, who strongly recommended that his friend Benjamin Maddock study Butler's *Analogy:* "you will derive much pleasure from Butler's Analogy, without exception the most unanswerable demonstration of the folly of infidelity that the world ever saw."¹⁸

The one apologist for Christianity whose works Kirke White would have to know at Cambridge was William Paley, whose *Evidences of Christianity* (1794) was a compulsory subject of study for all who wished to enter the university. Indeed, White read Paley's works quite early in life, for in the third essay of *Melancholy Hours* White has the goddess of Melancholy defend herself against the charge of idleness by asserting that she is no more useless than "were Plato and Socrates, Locke and Paley."[19] Paley was a pillar of the established Church in White's lifetime, and his last important book, *Natural Theology* (1805), was published only one year before White's death. This book would have had as great appeal to White as did Butler's *Analogy* because Paley pursues, in painstaking detail, an elaborate analogy between the designs of machinery and the design of the universe, between the anatomy of the human frame and the anatomy of nature. Paley proves that everywhere is evidence of a great design and that, consequently, there must be a great Designer—God. In the following passage from *Natural Theology* White could find the language of science explaining itself as also the language of God:

Whatever is done, God could have done without the intervention of instruments or means: but it is in the construction of instruments, in the choice and adaptation of means, that a creative intelligence is seen. It is this which constitutes the order and beauty of the universe. God, therefore, has been pleased to prescribe limits to his own power, and to work his ends within those limits. The general laws of matter have perhaps the nature of these limits; its inertia, its reaction; . . . the laws of magnetism, of electricity; and probably others, yet undiscovered.[20]

It is no wonder, then, that White shared an enthusiasm for knowledge with other young men, like Coleridge and Shelley, who also aspired to be great poets. Science was providing a new language of discourse, a fact which was in itself exciting to young writers; but more importantly to Coleridge, White, and countless others, science seemed not only compatible with the truths of religion but indeed it seemed to demonstrate those truths. At first White's ambition for education was a matter largely secular, but as he learned more and more he turned toward religious training. He increasingly identified his education with his religion, not only because he hoped for a livelihood from appointment in the Church but also because he needed the substance of knowledge as a ground for his religious hopes. In other words, his studies were pursued as a means for strengthening his religious faith, and his intellect was to be made into a tool of Christianity.

He saw education as a means of his liberation, for his bodily comfort as well as for his intellectual and spiritual health. He once argued that "the great excellence of religion and piety" was that "they not only lead to *eternal* happiness, but to the happiness of this world."[21] We know that he rebelled against the manual training of the loom, and we may speculate that his increasing desire to be released from his articles for a legal apprenticeship was in part the result of his discontent with the daily chores of a clerk's life. What Kirke White needed was food for his imagination and exercise for his intellectual powers. He is an example of the lower-class child of genius for whom no doors open easily into the great world of power and influence.

That White's poem on his own character should refer to political indecision is no surprise. There have been few periods of history so exciting for England than the two decades of Kirke White's life. It was a time of many able calls for political, social, and economic reform: Jeremy Bentham's *Introduction to Principles of Morals and Legislation* (1789) called for a reform of the legal system; Thomas Paine, in *The Rights of Man* (1791) and *The Age of Reason* (1794), encouraged a revolution in politics, economics, and religion; William Godwin's *Political Justice* (1793) was a powerful indictment of all government as contrary to human fulfillment; and Thomas Malthus's *Principles of Population* (1798) warned of the dangers of overpopulation and a diminishing supply of natural resources. The young Kirke White shared this current of enthusiasm for reform, writing that "the discovery of evil naturally leads us to contribute our mite towards the alleviation of the wretchedness it introduces."[22]

White's genius for poetry, his interest in the law, and his call to the ministry might sometimes conflict, but all were in agreement that the human condition stood in need of repair. Given his sympathies for downtrodden people, his silence concerning the revolution in France and the rise of Napoleon is strange, to say the least. Once he remarked on the military, if not political, state of affairs: on the occasion of a possible invasion in 1805, he wrote that "fervid patriotism" should "find an echo in every bosom in England," though "the voice of the Muses [may be] quite suspended in the clang of arms."[23] Robert Southey may have had something to do with silencing the young man and so saving him from the bad opinion of posterity, something Southey might have thought he should do when he edited Kirke White's papers after White's death in 1806.

That Kirke was interested in political matters is only slightly indicated in some of his letters. He wrote to Neville in June 1800 about an ugly affair of soldiers breaking up a benefit performance for Campbell (a "democrat").

> I had a ticket given me to the boxes, on Monday night, for the benefit of Campbell, from Drury-Lane, and there was such a riot as never was experienced here before. He is a democrat, and the soldiers planned a riot in conjunction with the *mob*. We heard the shouting of the rabble in the street before the *play* was over; the moment the curtain dropped, an officer went into the front box, and gave the word of command; immediately about sixty troopers started up, and six trumpeters in the pit played "God save the king." The noise was astonishing. The officers in the boxes then drew their swords; and at another signal the privates in the pit drew their bludgeons, which they had hitherto concealed, and attacked all indiscriminately, that had not a uniform: the officers did the same with their swords, and the house was one continued scene of confusion. . . . They then formed a troop, and having emptied the play-house, they scoured the streets with their swords, and returned home victorious.[24]

White's interest in this "astonishing" scene (though not very unusual for the times) is somewhat aloof. He was no longer inspired by the winds of democracy as he said he was in the poem he wrote when he was younger. Indeed, his only interest in the riot turns out to be that his law office became involved in the litigation: "we have informations in our office against the officers."[25] The passage, upon close reading, nevertheless shows that White is critical of the soldiers' behavior. His grounds of criticism are, however, civil rather than political. This episode and White's response illustrate a recurring theme in his life and works: his passion for order and his fear of chaos. He identified established government, established Church, and the structure of English law with an order which gave evidence of God's benevolent providence.

When events in his life worked out to his satisfaction, he felt that his faith in order was well founded, but when events failed, he was confused. His eagerness to study was also an anxiety for confirmation of his faith in order, but his personal experiences of vocational disappointments, failing health, emotional sympathies with dissenting Christianity, and, not least of all, his reading material from among the new poets of his time—all contributed to his melancholy reflection that order and harmony were either not characteristics of his world or that he was not fit to recognize them and would not be until he was educated. His hope and expectation was that a right education would equip him to recognize not only the real order of the universe but that he would also thereby find his proper place within that order. In the ninth essay of his *Melancholy Hours* he proposed "that the man who thinks deeply, especially if his reading be extensive, will . . . become habituated to a pensive . . . cast of thought." The pensive man will find, then, that he is "enveloped in mystery, and that the mystery of man's situation is not without alarming and fearful circumstances." But "the meditative man . . . [uses his] reasoning powers, and . . . [enlarges] his conceptions of the mysteries of his own existence" until he discovers that "a perfect harmony runs through all the parts of the universe" except in man himself.[26] To restore man to that harmony is the combined task of all human professions, from poet to priest. White knew from his own private experience that harmony was something to be sought, not something to be possessed. His dread of death with its threat of absolute disorder was a strong motive to transform the black melancholy of "Phrensy" into the white melancholy of "Contemplation."[27]

In a letter to Benjamin Maddock, written during the period when he was trying to arrange for financial support to attend the university, White admitted that "there is a species of morbid sensibility to which [he had] often been a victim, which preys upon [his] heart, and, without giving birth to one actively useful or benevolent feeling, does but brood on selfish sorrows, and magnify its own misfortunes." He continues in the same letter to speak of his "unworthiness" to become "a minister of Christ," and his unworthiness, he speculates, must be the result of his "pride" in his writing. He was experiencing a depression so great that he thought "at times, [he was] mad, and destitute of religion."[28] This depression was the result of his not having the means for going to the university, and so his misfortune was a punishment by God for his pride. As soon as his affairs were worked out so that he could go to Cambridge, he "returned thanks to God for this providential opening."[29]

Inspired by renewed hope, he felt prepared to explain to his brother "the real doctrines of the Church of England." White asserts that the soul is immortal and that its nature can be understood by analogy with intellectual processes: "this is what constitutes the human soul. It is an immaterial essence—no one knows what it consists of, or where it resides. . . . When we discuss a topic of cool reasoning, the process is carried on in the brain. . . . [W]hen we think, we move no organ: the reason depends on no action of matter, but seems as it were to hover over us." He is adopting a current means of argument for proving that "the soul is immaterial . . . to a mathematical demonstration."[30] Kirke White's greatest motive for education, we realize, was his need to reinforce the argument for spiritual immortality. For him there was a perfect compatibility between this motive and his other ones of securing a satisfying livelihood and doing God's will as a part of the cosmic design.

He admitted occasionally in his later correspondence that all was not fitting perfectly into the grand design. He had to overcome his fleshly temptations, especially sexual ones, to keep on his chosen course. He said to Ben Maddock that he would "never, never marry!" His reason was that his affections "are already engaged as much as they will ever be." He meant that his emotions were bound up with his intellectual commitments to the ministry and to poetry, not to persons. Then he said something that tells us how troubling all this was: "I love too ardently to make love innocent, and therefore I say farewell to it."[31] And, besides, he said, he did not want to try to raise a family in "narrow circumstances." White sometimes yielded to a temptation to identify sensuality with imagination, as he did when he condemned Moore's love poems for subverting the high aim of poetry, i.e., to encourage "the virtuous and the noble."[32]

As for his own imagination, he thought he must consider exchanging "the Muses for mathematics, and abstain from writing verses at least until [he] takes [his] degree." He reserved, however, the right to decide that later, after he knew if he would have time to "relax [him]self at intervals, with those delightful reveries which have hitherto formed the chief pleasure of [his] life." He knew that "the pursuit of Truth is a much more important business than the exercise of imagination," that he had to put Fancy behind him (however much he regretted doing so) and hope instead to "enjoy the sweet satisfaction of being useful . . . to [his] fellow-mortals."[33] Conflicts, then, continued in his life after his career at the university opened up: conflicts between a life of the mind and a life of the senses (and emotions), a life of the ministry and a life of poetry. His imagination would not let him rest, even while his reason worked overtime to subordinate all his experience to the great objective of his life: to make him "a fit herald for the important message [he was] ordained to deliver."[34] These conflicts lay behind his admission to Ben Maddock in September 1804 that he was "a singular being under a common outside; [he was] a profound dissembler of [his] inward feelings, and necessity has taught [him] the art."[35]

While at Cambridge White's application to study was frequently interrupted by his increasing illness. The cumulative effect was shattering: "I have had an attack of my old nervous complaint, and my spirits have been so wretchedly shattered, that my surgeon says I shall never be well till I have removed somewhere, where I can have society and amusement. It is a very distressing thing to be ill in college," he confided to his brother.[36] Later he wrote to Maddock that "a very slight over-stretch of the mind in the day-time occasions [him] not only a sleepless night, but a night of *gloom* and horror." In his distress at not being in better health, he confessed his growing inability to find consolation in his religion: "The Gog-magog hills for my body, and the Bible for my mind, are my only medicines. I am sorry to say, that neither are quite adequate."[37] The old "chaos of all contradiction" was returning in the guise of physical deterioration and spiritual doubt; within a few weeks of his death he grudgingly observed that "the cultivation of your mind is of minor importance to that of your heart, your temper, and disposition." He had to battle with his pride, his heart, temper, and disposition, while cultivating his mind, with the result that his life became like a "vessel . . . tossed about" so that it was a wonder he was "yet *upon* the waves."[38] Shortly before his death he told Maddock that his religious "progress had, if anything, been retrograde. [He was] still as dark, still as cold, still as ignorant, still as fond of the world, and [had] still fewer desires after holiness."[39] His learning had not, as he expected, much assisted his spiritual enlightenment; instead, his physical sufferings and desires for pleasure left him confused and unhappy, for his mind and spirit had gone in one direction while his body and emotions went in another. Left without a clear guide and purpose, his imagination, his power to create, began to feed upon itself.

III "In The Present Enlightened Age": His Literary Taste

Kirke White was a self-conscious heir of the Enlightenment, with its virtues of practical reason and its vices of empirical self-interest. But so was he an heir of the tensions which had been building between the *philosophes* and Christianity. His reading material was overwhelmingly the product of eighteenth-century Europe, especially England, although he was making rapid strides in other languages and cultures. His earliest reading must have been the Bible (which he cites once to illustrate a "perfect master-piece" of the sublime in literature), but very early in his life he discovered the poetry of Thomas Warton, the Younger, and Mark Akenside, both of whose works he admired and imitated in his own poetry. From the beginning of his literary interests, his taste inclined toward the poetry of sublimity. Warton "abounds in sublimity and loftiness of thought" and so he was preferred to Pope; Akenside and Thomson wrote much poetry with "instances of sublimity," and even though Robert Bloomfield's *Farmer's Boy* was "simply sweet," it had "no grandeur or height."[40]

Sublimity in poetry is the mark of its highest achievement, while sweetness is desirable only if it is pastoral. White's reading of poetry was mainly divided between the sublime kind of contemplative and meditative verse done by Warton and Akenside in imitation of Milton's "Il Penseroso," and the pastoral kind of delights in rural sweetnesses done by Bloomfield, and occasionally by Thomson, in the tradition of Milton's "L'Allegro." He read Johnson's *Lives of the Poets* and Burke's *Philosophical Enquiry into the Origins of Our Ideas of the Sublime and the Beautiful,* finding in both reinforcement of his taste for poetry of the sublime kind, though from Johnson he was also learning to be more demanding for a strong moral quality in "polite literature."[41] What he would not settle for was a poetry of pretty sounds: "in the present enlightened age, I think it will not be disputed that mere jingle and sound ought invariably to be sacrificed to sentiment and expression."[42]

The "sentiment" he preferred was moral thoughtfulness, religious reflection that "raises the soul above the evils incident to life."[43] The "expression" he preferred was "native dignity and simplicity, without art, and without ornament," which would produce "the true sublime."[44] "High sounding words, or pompous magnificence" will not accomplish sublimity, nor will "harmonious modulations and unvarying exactness of measure"; the latter qualities "have reduced our fashionable poetry to mere sing-song." White joined a growing company of critics who blamed Alexander Pope for having introduced such refinements into English poetry that Milton's "nerve and pathos" had generally disappeared. Thomas Warton brought Milton's virtues back to English poetry; he practiced "the sombre descriptive," that is, he "overcasts his descriptions" with "gloomy tints" which help to "convey the most sublime ideas of the mind."[45] These "most sublime ideas" were the main subject of the series of essays Kirke White published in 1801 under the heading of *Melancholy Hours*.

His definition of "melancholy" is strongly derivative from Thomas Warton and John Milton, but "melancholy" is the state of mind that White believed necessary for cultivating the best literary taste. He looked for the literature that produced melancholy in its readers, for in that state one is best able to assert his humanity over against the multitude of evils in a world that seems bent upon perverting or destroying human values. Melancholy rises from "the contemplation of the miseries incident to life, and the evils which obtrude themselves upon society, and interrupt the harmony of nature." White's aim was to acquire the philosophic habit of mind, to become "the man who has attained that calm equanimity which qualifies him to look down upon the petty evils of life with indifference; who can so far conquer the weakness of nature, as to consider the sufferings of the individual of little moment, when put in competition with the welfare of the community, [for he is] alone the true philosopher."[46] Melancholy is the stimulus for both intellectual and imaginative activity: "So far from being idle, my mind is ever on the wing in the regions of fancy or that true philosophy which opens the book of human nature, and raises the soul above the evils incident to life."[47]

For the young man of sixteen to set out in life "with the design of discovering where [he] can best unite both objects: enjoyment the most exquisite, with virtue the most perfect,"[48] the journey would be treacherous indeed, as he himself imagined when he tried to put the case for pessimism (as he might have read in *Rasselas*) through the invention of a saturnine character in the twelfth *Melancholy Hour*. But in 1801 the young man's optimism was too strong, and his twelfth issue ends with a fainthearted and episodic tale by the pessimist, a tale that is not finished. The verve of these papers in 1801 is the result of White's enthusiastic interpretation of melancholy as the product of contemplation and fancy, in which "we . . . are enabled to contemplate our being, in all its bearings, and in its full extent, and the result is, that superiority to common views, and indifference to the things of this life, which should be the fruit of all *true* philosophy, and which, therefore, are the more peculiar fruits of that system of philosophy which is called the Christian."[49] Not only did he search out the literature of melancholy, then, but he was ambitious to write his own poems in the sublime mood of melancholy and therefore "contribute to the great end, and draw [the] soul from its sphere, to fix it on its Maker and Redeemer."[50] The most successful of the new poets to express the sublime were, in White's own estimate, "Wordsworth, Southey, and Coleridge . . . [who succeeded in uniting] richness of language, and warmth of coloring, with simplicity and pathos."[51] These were men whose company as poets Henry Kirke White was ambitious to join.

CHAPTER 2

Melancholy Hours: *Solitary Effusions to the Public*

THAT Kirke White should desire to write in the genre of the periodical essay in 1801 is far from surprising to the student of literary history. Since at least the last two decades of the seventeenth century in England, this genre had not only been popular with a wide audience, but it was also a form practiced by some of the best writers of prose that the language has to boast. While the models of essay writing by Bacon and Cowley from the seventeenth century may have set high standards of achievement for their heirs in the genre, it was more likely that the special features of the eighteenth-century periodical essay derived from the journalistic forms developed by Ned Ward's *London Spy* (1698–1700), with its descriptions of daily life in London, and most superbly by the *Tatler* and the *Spectator* (1709–1711, and 1711–1712), written mainly by Joseph Addison and Richard Steele. Mixing reportage with essays of argument and opinion, character analysis with literary criticism, Addison and Steele practically created a special genre of English prose; it was a kind of writing that could appeal to an audience with many tastes and a variety of interests, such as the British reading public was rapidly becoming in the eighteenth century.

The most important writers in this genre, as far as Kirke White's interest went, were Samuel Johnson and Oliver Goldsmith. White wrote his brother in 1800 that he had "got the Citizen of the World, Idler, Goldsmith's Essays, and part of the Rambler."[1] Johnson's *Rambler* papers were published originally in periodical form, between March 1750 and March 1752; his essays appeared in the *Idler* from April 1758 to April 1760. Using the popular device of pretending to be a foreign (Chinese) visitor commenting on the strange customs of the English, Goldsmith first published his *Citizen of the World* essays in the *Public Ledger* between January 1760 and August 1761; his articles from various magazines and newspapers were collected into a single volume as *Essays by Mr. Goldsmith* and published in 1765. Naturally, White's enthusiasm for this kind of writing was generated by his reading such masters of the language as Johnson and Goldsmith. White makes frequent mention of both authors, and his own essays show an imitation of their styles and subjects.[2]

Like Johnson, White sets out in his *Melancholy Hours* to teach his readers, and especially to teach them standards of good taste and the wisdom of piety. White imitates Johnson by dwelling (in poetry as well as in prose) on themes of death as "this universal medicine of the mind," as Johnson calls it in *Rambler* No. 17, where Johnson explains that "the frequent contemplation of death . . . shows the vanity of all human good."[3] Imitations of Goldsmith occur with perhaps even more frequency in White's prose, where the younger man echoes the older in such subjects as the progress of knowledge, sketches of moral qualities (such as friendship), and the advantages of traveling. In both Johnson and Goldsmith, White had before him persons who had, like himself, to overcome great social and economic disadvantages in order to pursue their callings as writers. White had to be particularly sensitive to advice such as the following, from Goldsmith's *Citizen of the World*:

> Books, my son, while they teach us to respect the interests of others, often make us unmindful of our own; while they instruct the youthful reader to grasp at social happiness, he grows miserable in detail, and attentive to universal harmony, often forgets that he himself has a part to sustain in the concert. . . . A youth who has thus spent his life among books, new to the world, and unacquainted with man but by philosophic information, may be considered a being, whose mind is filled with the vulgar errors of the wise; utterly unqualified for a journey through life, yet confident of his own skill in the direction, he sets out with confidence, blunders on with vanity, and finds himself at last undone.[4]

On the subject of melancholy White "sets out with confidence" and, certainly as Johnson would have said if Goldsmith had not, "blunders on with vanity." In Johnson's opinion, melancholy is an affliction of the mind not to be courted but rather to be combated with all the resources at one's disposal. On this subject Boswell and Johnson often disagreed, as Boswell reports several times in his *Life of Johnson* (1791): Johnson warned Boswell that "if it be the business of a wise man to be happy, it is foolish to indulge [melancholy]; and if it be a duty to preserve our faculties entire for their proper use, it is criminal." But, Boswell says, Johnson "was, I always thought, erroneously inclined to confound together [melancholy and madness]."[5] White, writing of melancholy, inherits Boswell's disposition to treat it as a phenomenon separate from madness, although behind Johnson's definition there was a long and distinguished tradition of calling it a disease of the mind.

Melancholy is a word early used in medicine to describe a condition of having too much "black bile," one of the four humours in the body; this is a condition marked by sullenness and gloomy anger. As such it is used by Shakespeare in *Julius Caesar* to account for errors of judgment: "O hateful Error, Melancholy's child, / Why dost thou show to the apt thoughts of men / The things that are not?" (V, iii, 67-69). In this same sense that melancholy persons are subject to illusions of danger, Johnson warns in *Rasselas* that "the superstitious are often melancholy, and the melancholy almost always superstitious" (Chapter 46). At its worst, melancholy may be a symptom of despair and so it is a kind of religious melancholy which Robert Burton examines in the third part of his *Anatomy of Melancholy* (1621); those who suffer from the "defect" of melancholy (such as atheists and hypocrites) are understandably liable to despair, but some "sincere Christians" less understandably suffer from a similar symptom—these are persons for whom Burton feels a deep sympathy; others suffer from an "excess" of melancholy (such as religious enthusiasts and fanatics for ceremony and ritual), but all such persons are suffering from mental sickness that Burton describes as a tool of Satan.

Against that understanding of *melancholy* held by many from Burton to Johnson there was another, to which Boswell inclined and which Kirke White accepts. This other use of the word intends by it a description of thought made sorrowful by contemplation and meditation. Milton makes this use of the word in *Il Penseroso* (1632) when he hails Melancholy as a "Goddess, sage and holy":

> Hail divinest Melancholy,
> Whose Saintly visage is too bright
> To hit the Sense of human sight;
> And therefore to our weaker view,
> O'erlaid with black, staid Wisdom's hue. (12-16)

This use of the word is much older than Milton, and it was much used in this way by many writers after Milton, including Thomas Warton, the Younger ("The Pleasures of Melancholy," 1747), James Thomson (*The Castle of Indolence*, 1748), and Samuel Rogers (*The Pleasures of Memory*, 1792). Kirke White, steeped in the poetry of Milton, Thomson, and the Wartons, champions the philosophical health of melancholy and sets out to rescue its reputation in his own *Melancholy Hours*.

In this series of essays he reveals that his writing is a search for the "power" that can raise one above the "petty evils of life."[6] Yearning to escape "irksome" circumstances, to attain a height of "sublimity" from which he could "look down" upon the sad and dusty ways of life, he obsessively employs metaphors and images of height and depth in his writing. The main advantage, or pleasure, of melancholy is that it can relieve the anxieties of coping with pettiness and dullness in everyday living, and so it is a state of mind for which everyone should hope and from which everyone could benefit. It is the mission of "sons of genius," artists of all kinds, to make clear the advantages of melancholy and, moreover, to invoke its virtue for the modern audience, which has a claim to happiness that can be satisfied by melancholy in the service of God and nature. In his first essay, White makes the winning appeal that all men can become philosophers; he suggests how that can be accomplished, and he explains why it should be an aim of all mankind.

I *The Pleasures of Melancholy*

The first essay defines melancholy as a product of imagination, as the embodiment of power, experienced as sublimity, and the cause of pleasure. White's ostensible object is to convince his reader that everyone, not only philosophers and poets, should benefit from the advantages of melancholy. He explores the paradoxical experience that melancholy is a cause of bliss as well as sorrow. From the outside, melancholy seems forbidding, but for the one possessed by it, melancholy is very beneficial. The lover, the unfortunate, and the disappointed man of ambition derive pleasure from melancholy, but theirs is nothing compared with that of the philosopher. The true philosopher feels a calm equanimity and indifference to the petty evils of life.

White knows that the word *melancholy* is an important one for his time, and he attempts to come to terms with its significance. To realize its power, one must divest himself of ordinary postures, as philosophers have when they, like the poets, "descant . . . on the pleasures of Melancholy" (p. 390). This divestiture occurs when one is able to "imagine" himself as having "risen above" the crowds of people: "I imagine myself placed upon an eminence above the crowds who pant below in the dusty tracks of wealth and honour" (p. 391). This is the essential first act of the man of melancholy: to *imagine* himself as set apart, special, abstracted from the petty concerns of the world. In such words we can hear a young man impatient with the constraints of his economically and socially depressed world, but no less can we understand that his is a voice for his readers who share his need to imagine themselves abstracted from the boorish, petty life into which most are born and wear out their existence.

The power of the individual mind, of imagination, is something analogous with, if not stimulated by, the power of all nature. Thus one may find in himself a power correspondent with that of the nature surrounding him: "when the howling storm rages in the heavens, the rain pelts on my roof, and the winds whistle through the crannies of my apartment, I feel the divine mood of melancholy upon me" (p. 391). The energy of nature so expressed releases in the imaginative man a similar if not identical power of motion and force; it can raise him to "an eminence" of vision, a place of calm and still serenity from which he can contemplate the scenes of human endeavor below him. The energy which raises the melancholy man is experienced as a "mood" of mind identifying not with the forms, but rather with the force of nature. In this mood one may escape the constraints of form to express a greater freedom of speculation. It is an experience which, for Kirke White, falls somewhere between the "pensive delight in nature's melancholy aspects" that he read in the poetry of the Wartons,[7] and the "presence that disturbs," the "sense sublime" that "impels / All thinking things" which

White could have read about in *The Lyrical Ballads* when he was thirteen years of age. White may be read as a figure on the boundary of a culture passing from the "age of Sensibility" to the "era of Romanticism."

Only the sublime vision can perceive the predicament of mankind. Any other attempt to understand will be doomed to failure by egotism, shortsightedness, and weary impatience. When one is involved in the irksome toils of livelihood, in "the vexations of business," he cannot see the errant ways of humankind and he may therefore save himself from the pain of recognizing error and falsehood, but he will also deprive himself of the pleasures of truth, and these pleasures are as sure signs of melancholy as are the more obvious signs of sorrow. To get at these special pleasures, one must move through the middle zone of indifference, out of the first stage of anxiety and vexation, but thereby into the final stage of "ecstatic bliss" and "delight" of contemplation available to the spectator alone, to the man of melancholy who, like the author and hopefully the reader of these essays, can find amusement in relaxation, "when the mind . . . sinks into itself for a moment of solitary ease," where one can remove himself from "the anxieties of an irksome employment" and find a release for "the fervour of a glowing mind" (p. 393).

White's requirements for the free play of thought that can discover truth only when it can escape the bondage of flesh are requirements that Shaftesbury had also demanded for the aesthetic function of philosophy. Shaftesbury sought, as Cassirer explains, "the true theodicy, the ultimate justification of existence, not in the sphere of joy and sorrow but in that of the free inner activity of forming according to a purely intellectual prototype and archetype."[8] To compare White's notion of intellectual activity with Shaftesbury's is not to suggest that White's is sophisticated, but merely to point out the heritage of thought which White has to work out his own position. The key point of similarity is in the notion of "the free inner activity" that White also believes to mark the man of melancholy.

White needed to find a place of calm and "solitary ease," taking him from the dreary labors of his irksome existence. He expresses a growing discontent among the lower classes in England with their dreary lives, and so his youthful essays in definition are articulations of a cultural development as well as the explorations of a concept by a budding poet. His obsession with heights and power is a trait we often notice in Kirke White's writings, but we should not dismiss this as a symptom only of youthful ambition and adolescent yearning; rather, we should consider that his appeal to so large an audience would occur in part because he voiced a yearning and an ambition of a class of people in England and in America, a class which knew all too well the dreariness of life in "dusty tracks," preoccupied with the "petty evils of life," but sensitive to the virtue of "silent walks" and "solitary effusions." Society may be a maze of misdirection, but within the individual imagination lay a power for rising above that maze, discerning the plan of harmony implied by nature's self, and creating the structures of art whereby others might rise to the same height of vision and thereby recover the direction which will bring mankind back into the harmony originally established by the will of God. The melancholy person is the person of imagination, empowered to see largely, to experience sublimity, and therefore be admitted to the pleasures of truth in possibilities as well as burdened by the sorrows of truth in errant actualities.

II Sons of Genius

Those who realize, or become conscious of, their power of imagination to experience melancholy are, in a favorite phrase of White's, "sons of genius." He takes the term of "genius" as synonymous with "power," and specifically the power of imagination. These sons of genius are marked by their mood of melancholy, a gift often misconstrued by those who have not yet discovered it for themselves. In four of his essays, White explores and defines the predicaments of these sons of genius living in modern times. He observes that most are predestined to struggle unnoticed, that their inspiration ("genius") of melancholy is publicly abused, that they are driven into isolation by vanity and falsehood, and that they must learn to suffer all these hardships with patience and resignation. White explores these themes in these four essays mainly by using the device of anecdote: he narrates, in No. 2, the story of an acquaintance many of whose problems are clearly those of White himself; in No. 3, he uses the device of a dream-vision to put on trial the virtues of Melancholy; in No. 4, he fabricates a tale of personal misadventure in friend-hunting that might very well be a confession of White's own efforts to find patrons and sponsors for his education and / or writing; and, in No. 12, he invents a tale of exotic wandering, in the manner of Johnson's *Rasselas,* when a young traveler spends an evening with a philosophic ("melancholy") hermit in his mountain cave.

Sons of Genius, White says in No. 2, are predestined to struggle unnoticed (a theme made extraordinarily popular by Thomas Gray's "Elegy Written in a Country Churchyard," and one always appealing to the young Kirke White, unnoticed himself — the very epitome of Gray's poem, as many an Englishman must have believed himself to be). Who knows how many more young geniuses will rest "his head upon the lap of Earth / A youth to fortune and to fame unknown?" Our essayist tells us that he knows personally of one such, named Charles Wanely, who was orphaned at the age of sixteen years. He was then articled to an attorney (like White, of course). He found it very difficult to go from his pleasure in reading the classics to reading dull, tedious law books. He was sensitive to what he considered to be a condescending attitude by the attorney to whom he was articled. He was angered and humiliated by this attitude, and decided after one particular episode to leave the community, his home, forever. He is imagined as he set out, tracking a hill, resting to cast one look backward over his home town, and in this special attitude, Charles Wanely comes close to the sublime experience; having risen above his lowly beginnings, he can experience melancholy pleasure while casting his last look upon his childhood home.

The essayist came across Charles Wanely five years later. While visiting the Continent, he was strolling a street in Naples when he suddenly encountered an Improvisatori upon a moonlit night. While observing the Italian performer, the narrator suddenly noticed the face of an emaciated man in the audience — it may have been Charles Wanely. The effect was sensational: the vision caused the narrator to feel stupefied with surprise; the object of his vision, Charles Wanely, disappeared. If, as the essay tells us, "the principal end of man is to arrive at happiness" (p. 395), then one must not follow the route of Charles Wanely, for he seems not to have found the "principal end." White allows us to believe that happiness is to be found in contemplating the melancholy end of such persons as Charles Wanely, preventing us from falling into the same errors of isolation and anonymity. The scene in Naples, moonlit and filled with surprise, is a moment of discovery, when the narrator realizes that Charles Wanely does not represent the best way to deal with the adversities of existence: "Nobody knew him. Nobody had ever seen such a person" (p. 397). This is what Kirke White needed to believe for himself and what he wanted his readers to believe for themselves. Charles Wanely deserves the fate he chose for himself—a fate of nonentity. Charles Wanely is what the reader must not become, though his life is a cause for melancholy reflection.

In Essay No. 3, the speaker takes a midnight ramble by the riverside, where he is halted by the music of a flute, which soothes his thoughts of indignation at the evils of man. Its music ravishes the listener. After the music stops, imagination is excited so that during the narrator's sleep a dream-vision is stimulated. In this vision the dreamer imagines himself in an arena with many spectators. There is a throne at one end, and on it sits a female divinity who is clothed in azure and has a sun on her forehead whose radiance illumines the whole arena. She seems forbidding at a distance, but she is mild when viewed from close up. She has blue, piercing eyes; she is intelligent and awesome, but she is reassuring. She is the goddess of Wisdom and she now (in the dream) reigns on earth. She is here to try the followers of Folly. And at this moment a suspect is being brought to trial: she is veiled in black, but the dreamer recognized her as a favorite goddess—Melancholy!

Thus does Kirke White translate his concern for philosophy, for unpopular learning, into a mock trial in which the very forces of nature are witnesses of truth. The sun itself is Wisdom, while the river and the skylark are the incensed witnesses against false accusation. The dreamer is a sympathizer with misguided mankind, but he is above all a friend of Philosophy, the former name of Melancholy, daughter of Misfortune and Virtue. But most important, White presents Melancholy as a gift of God, a gift of comfort in times of difficulty. White is searching for a mythic accounting of melancholy, just as so many of his admired poets, such as the Wartons and Collins, had done; this was an era when, as Sister M. Kevin Whelan has said, "melancholy becomes for the enthusiast a being of divinity somewhat akin to Fancy."[9] White is suggesting that melancholy, a world sorrow, is the daughter of God, gift of Heaven, force of truth, but also the same force (though different in name) for pagan as for Christian: Magnanimity or Charity. She is constantly on trial in a fallen world, but she will always be vindicated by wisdom and nature.

A true son of genius, one who can benefit from the lessons of melancholy, is one who learns not to put his trust in his fellow man, one who learns to withdraw from dependence upon his fellow creature, no stronger and possibly weaker than himself. This is the point of Essay No. 4, that friend-hunters are like fortune-hunters: men who make it their business to acquire friends, hoping to benefit from their influence, will discover that this can be a galling experience. A friend thus acquired can make one a slave of his caprice. The essayist turns narrator once again to illustrate his point with an example from his own life, for he too was once (and only once, he emphasizes) a friend-hunter.

White's narrative of friend-hunting may reflect something of his own discovery that humiliation follows sycophancy, but he tells this story mainly to make the point that such a melancholy conclusion is consistent with the lessons of all nature. For the falsity of friends is like any other fact of nature; man is naturally a selfish creature from whom disinterested friendship requires extraordinary effort, extraordinary self-discipline, perhaps the grace of imagination itself—what White here calls Melancholy. This truth is something, like friend-hunting itself, which cannot be merely invoked or told to another (for who can preach philosophy to the mob?); instead, it must be experienced by each one for himself. Those who discover the truths of melancholy, those true sons of genius, will become reclusive in their habits retreating to solitary living where their only companions may be creatures of the lower kind. Montaigne had his cat, and the narrator has his dog, "Bob," who sits at this moment surveying him while he writes his story down. This then is the only hope for a friend, one who has not the selfish nature of mankind, one who is not blessed with the gift of reason.

Essay No. 4 thus ends on a note of ambivalence, whether cynically or satirically, to reduce the human spirit from aspiration to contentment with animal companionship. Surely, however, a philosophical person need not retire so far from the human community in order to achieve "some little eminence" (p. 407). White will hardly maintain this position with consistency, but there is little doubt that he suffered occasional pains of misanthropy while passing into his adolescence. The world of man was sufficient evidence, for him, that all was not right with God's creation; indeed, the ways of man were certain proof that the Christian view of things was the correct one. Each of these essays contributes in its own small way to the accumulating evidence that proves White's point, that "man is naturally a selfish creature, and it is only by the aid of philosophy that he can so far conquer the defects of his being, as to be capable of disinterested friendship. *Who*, then, can expect to find that benign disposition" that White's essayist searches for (p. 407)? His search for an answer takes him, in Essay No. 12, to visit the residence of a hermit, one of those recluses described at the conclusion of No. 4.

No. 12, telling a tale of a hermit and a traveler, was the last in White's series, drawing his argument to its philosophic conclusion, as though the essayist were, like the young traveler of this last essay, completing his pilgrimage in search of truth. It can be noted here, however, because it clearly fits this early pattern of describing sons of genius as those who achieve the melancholy vision at the cost of separation and alienation, however high and eminent that achievement might appear. We are taken in No. 12 to a distant and mysterious land, to a cave on a hillside near the ancient city of Byzantium. There lived a certain hermit who was undervalued by the natives of the region because he was not austere enough to suit their strict and superstitious religion.

The essay ends abruptly, as if White intended to add another installment—which he never did. His own life and writing reflect this combination of the traveler and the hermit: one searching for the happiness that combines enjoyment with virtue, the other satisfied that we are not meant to be happy on this earth, that enjoyment must be postponed and virtue can be found only in a life of denial and selflessness. These are the usual contradictory forces that create tension in White's life and in his poetry, although they are probably not unusual symptoms for any young person of talent and intelligence. His youth impelled him to search (and to hope for the kind of fulfillment that could be represented for a youthful man in the image of a "woman with a mind"), to explore and gather experience, while his training, his culture, his inherited code of values told him that Christianity was the fulfillment already available, present to deny the values of those experiences touted by youthful ambition and imagination. We should be alert in his poetry for images of traveling, movement, searching, exploration, cities, streams, and warmth, set against contrary images of stasis, retreat, withdrawal, caves, mountain tops, stone, deserts, and cold; these make up his terrain of imaginative discourse.

If Kirke White's youthful expectations prove to be correct, what he learns from Christianity will resolve the tensions set up by his youthful contradictions between knowledge and faith, exploration and retreat, pleasure and virtue. He will make a mighty effort in his study and in his writing to achieve the resolution promised by Christianity. This mighty effort is a function of his imagination quite as much as it is a promise of his reason, although both his imagination and reason are conditioned by, if not the gifts of, a special genius attending all who achieve the vision of melancholy.

III   *Our Modern Muses*

In this next group of essays, White explores a topic dear to his youthful ambition: the plight and prospects for young genius, and in particular for young poets (like himself). In No. 5 he argues that the sonnet is a form especially adapted to the taste of the melancholy man; in No. 6 he suggests that few legitimate poets have ever managed to emerge from hereditary obscurity; in No. 8 he discourses on the subject of inscriptive writings; and in No. 10 he celebrates the talents of Robert Southey as an experimenter in versification. Underlying all of these essays is not only the obvious concern with modern poetry but the less obvious concern with premature burial for the modern muse, the cultural ignorance of genius that manifests itself in the arts, and the desperation of true poets who must utilize forms that appeal to modern tastes, reach out to the living as though they were themselves among the dead, and risk condemnation for being unique and bold.

Essay No. 5 is a surprising argument, beginning as it does with the assertion that the sonnet is especially adapted to the taste of the Melancholy Man, but ending with the even more vigorous assertion that the English poet should renounce the sonnet as a form not conducive to the expression of English genius. In its favor, especially for the Melancholy Man, the sonnet cannot become tiresome because of its brevity, because its form accords well with the feeling of dejection, and because its elegiac delicacy and plaintiveness accord with melancholy sentiments. White traces the history of this poetic form in English, attempting to understand why it has become lately popular after a long period of disfavor. He finds that fifty years earlier the sonnet had been repugnant to the English, because, he speculates, the earlier sonneteers had imitated the Italian models too closely, making it into a metaphysical conceit when it did not lend itself well to that form of expression.

Voicing a youthful enthusiasm, if not an Anglophilic provincialism, White calls upon modern poets to renounce the Italian form altogether. English poets already labor beneath enough restrictions that they should not be tied as well by a blind regard for Continental precedent, especially when it was probably set by some wandering bards of France (i.e., Provençal poets). He would not have the English abandon the fourteen-line poem, but he would have them surrender the name of "sonnet" in order to establish the English form as independent of the Italian, to gain some independence of expression for a form which is the result of individual power, not the false advantage of Continental tradition. Finally, the English must find another name for the "quatorzain" or banish it from the language. Thus does the young poet strike out for an independent voice, recognizing the power of English "sonnets" but protesting that they should not be read against the tradition of Italian and French sonnets, for the English poem has a power of sentiment and expression that will not be subordinated to musical effects and indeed cannot be subordinated if it will succeed at all.

The theme of independent power, asserted in defiance of conventions and rules, is frequent in White's writing. Margery Bailey's description of Edward Young might apply as well to Kirke White: "his characteristic work shows a vigorous individual straining at the bonds of correctness and regularity, and often breaking through them to assert himself. . . . There was in Edward Young a good deal of Prometheus bound."[10] In neither case, we may think, was the bondage finally broken, although in the example of White a true test was not to be possible because of his early death. The "straining" may be more clear in White's essays than in his poetry, but even there we shall see how he, again like Young, uses forms that are conventional and stiff while trying to break through them "to assert himself."

This comes naturally to him, realizing as he does that he must combat the adversity of his circumstances without the benefit of class privilege. The English poet who makes his own way, using the natural strengths of his native language, giving voice to his unique power that breaks through the jingle of Continental song—this is the type of writer White celebrates and believes himself capable of becoming.

In Essay No. 6 he explores the theme of natural genius struggling against hereditary obscurity. He acknowledges that poetry needs the encouragement of culture and attention, that it is a blossom of delicate growth, unlike mathematics or mechanics, which require strength and a certain insensibility. It is painful to reflect how many a nameless bard now lies dead, how many have never been heard whose talents might have benefited from some of the leisure so many have wasted. Those who are conscious of their real merit lost or buried in a culture that rewards mediocrity, those are the ones who need melancholy to survive with dignity, for they are tempted into misanthropic discontent and early death. The want of leisure and comfort leaves talented persons mourning and languishing.

This is something all his readers will admit, and so White points with admiration to the two outstanding instances of successful achievement by men of talent without leisure or comfort from their social circumstances. Those two are the brothers Bloomfield, Robert and Nathaniel. The author of the famous *Farmer's Boy* has already received the applause he deserves, but his brother Nathaniel has yet to receive his due recognition. He in fact suffers from the success of his famous brother, because Englishmen too easily become inured to the novel and the unique, cannot endure a repetition of the uncommon, and will believe it is not fashionable to continue to patronize indigent merit. Therefore, Kirke White touts Nathaniel Bloomfield as a poet who deserves attention, one whose name would be honored if critics value bold and vivid images in the service of original conceptions.

Whether it be Nathaniel Bloomfield or Robert Southey, the poet whose accomplishments most excite White's admiration is the one who challenges tradition, overcomes the adversities of time and circumstance, and expresses his unique voice in a time of conventions and mediocrity. Citing the examples of the

Bloomfields, he writes in Essay No. 6 of these "two illustrious instances of poverty *bursting* through the cloud of surrounding impediments into the full blaze of notoriety and *eminence*" (p. 416; my italics). We realize when we notice his use of such metaphors (mainly tropes of violence) that White is himself yearning with a similar desire to burst to some eminence in the esteem of men. It is the distinctive mark of all his writing. And in no essay of this series does this yearning become more obvious than in No. 8, which takes up the popular subject of inscriptive writing. In this essay, the young essayist takes on a stolid tradition (as he had done when he criticized the sonnet tradition) but he also, and more boldly, challenges one of the most popular poets of the day, William Hayley.

He takes on a tradition when he contends that much has been said on the subject of inscriptive writings, but little of it has been to much purpose. White proposes to test this kind of verse against Boileau's definition, that "les inscriptions doivent etre simples, courtes, et familiéres" (p. 425). Few, even of the best, inscriptions can satisfy this definition; Akenside's classic imitations are beautiful, but they are not simple, short or familiar; and Southey's inscriptions are noble, but they are better in a book than on a column or cenotaph. When one visits the tomb of an illustrious person he expects writing which is nervous, concise, and impressive; he will turn away from the conceits of the epigrammatist and the tedious prolixity of the herald. The writer of inscriptions must not try to use words for what they cannot accomplish, i.e., excite the mind to an effervescence of the sublimer affections; he must limit his effort to use words for pointing feelings which already exist in the reader toward a beneficial purpose.

What the essayist wants from inscriptive writing is greater decorum, more responsibility, and respect for the audience. In this kind of writing White emphasizes the need to subordinate individuality and personal expression to a greater need, the celebration of public virtue and generosity. Experiments in inscriptive writing are useful to the young poet, for they require him to develop a consciousness of responsibility to his audience that otherwise he might ignore. He must pay attention to local and topical propriety, and he must use his craft to provoke reflection in the reader, leaving him a better person. These reflections must not be prolonged; they should be hints rather than dissertations, just sufficient to start an idea and let the reader's imagination carry it out to completion.

In Essay No. 10, however, White applauds Robert Southey for his successful experiments in versification. It is no wonder that Robert Southey might be flattered by the attentions of this young man of genius, for in him the elder poet could find a respect for his own poetic objectives that few others at the time were showing. And we must remember that for White, Robert Southey was the foremost member of an exciting new group of English poets, the group that included Wordsworth and Coleridge—experimenters and champions of romantic sensibility. Thus, while we might raise an eyebrow at White's particular choice of Southey over the others, we must remember that for White to notice any one of them is a tribute to his good taste and sensitivity, in principle if not in every application. Those features of Southey's poem *Thalaba the Destroyer* which White points out for admiration are features that generally White looks for in the best of modern verse: innovation, novelty, detailed observation, and bold discrimination. These qualities must, however, be functions of other, more traditional, principles of poetry: propriety and genius.

Not all experimenters in versification have been so successful as Southey, although some great English poets have been experimenters, including Sidney, Spenser, and Donne. While these great poets deserve admiration, White believes they have not been so successful as the moderns, especially Southey and Bowles, in achieving grace while exploring remarkably wide areas of versification. One of the reasons White likes Southey's poetry, especially his experimental poetry, is that White knows Southey will be met with much critical disapprobation and even more reader disapproval—which is what the young poet knows he is up against himself. He therefore likes to flatter his own genius with the example of others in whom he can see himself one day, others who will take on fearlessly the enemy against which the fledgling writer himself wishes to battle. Southey is White's alter ego, if not his spiritual father, a hero of the young man's new aesthetic. White is searching for a voice of his own, a way to distinguish himself in an adverse world, but until he achieves it for himself he studies and touts the achievements of those who have found unique ways—like Robert Southey. At first the reader will find innovative poetry uncouth, but will after perusal discover it is sweet and graceful, *if* it is an expression of genuine feeling, truthfully rendered with a strong sense of fitness.

Whenever White seems closest to undisciplined enthusiasm for the novel and the sensational, he always pulls up short, takes stock of his subject and his response to it, and finally tempers the enthusiasm with a strong dose of correction. He insists that genius be free to express itself, but not free of all the tools of art which he needs to make that expression. The genius in poetry must learn his craft, must study his audience, must absorb his ancestors into himself, and then, but only then, may he be truly free to express himself in a new, but fitting and appropriate, voice. *Thalaba* seems to White to provide a nice example of such an accomplishment; it combines an abrupt sublimity of transitions with a sublime simplicity of manner; its wild freedom of versification is appropriate to its romantic story; it combines an uncommon versification with delicate touches of narrative; and, finally, it has the desired effect of wild irregularity because it uses conventional devices with bold discrimination. White looks for and finds what we might not be able to admit as features of *Thalaba*, but he is looking for the right things to help him become an artist. Southey is for White the mentor that Coleridge found in Bowles, and, later, that Keats would find in Leigh Hunt.

IV *Claims of Happiness for God and Nature*

The "modern muse" lays a heavy assignment on the man of genius: he must not only entertain (e.g., write "jingling" sonnets), but he must also instruct (e.g., subordinate sound to sense). Discovering that precious balance is the major challenge for all artists, but how much more difficult it must be when the audience's expectations seem to be changing and uncertain; on the other hand, when all mankind seems teetering on the edge of cultural darkness, staring political and economic chaos in the face, benumbed by a paradoxical combination of daily tedium and epochal upheaval, of physical exhaustion and political excitement, of spiritual turpitude and intellectual revival, the time is much in need of both the entertainment and the instruction that the liberal and fine arts promise. Such was the era into which Kirke White was born and lived out his short life, an era whose paradoxical characteristics were keenly observed by Wordsworth at the beginning and by Shelley at the end; the Romantic poet realized that he must make the tedium of daily life into a romance of significance, that he must relocate the center of meaning from the world outside the self to the world within the self, if he was to have any chance of making art work to keep culture and the human spirit alive. In three of his essays, Nos. 7, 9, and 11, Kirke White attempts to address the problems he finds in his world, though his terms of understanding are conventional and his solutions may seem even more conventional.

While the perplexities of existence are quite as complicated for the thoughtful man as for the unthinking creature pursuing his daily comforts, for the young man Kirke White life seems tolerable only if it is meaningful, and it cannot be meaningful only in material terms, which are too fleeting and uncertain to depend upon. His own great anxiety is to escape an imprisoning and limiting vision of existence to which the merely materialistic life, either in its goals or in its means, condemns one. We should be sensitive to his use of such words as "envelope," "intervene," "cloud," "overwhelm," and "blind"; these are qualities of an existence which is imaged forth in such terms as the grave, boundaries, sublunary states, and floods of misery. His view of existence is thus one of darkened, sunken, engulfed consciousness when weighed down by the burdens and cares of material and temporal preoccupation.

The philosophical man of mind will rise above the flood, dissipate the clouds, clarify his vision, and see the light of truth that shines steady and distant from the teeming, anxious, busy world of getting, spending, surviving for the day. As David B. Morris has pointed out, "the sublime always implied the possibility of rising above the ordinary limitations of humanity to a vision of wholeness or to a passionate experience of the mysterious."[11] White is too much a man of reason, albeit of *faith* in reason, to abandon his search for truth and yield instead to the obscurity of "the mysterious." Mystery, a function of ignorance, may impel the young seeker on his way to truth, but surely mystery is not to be the *result*, the *goal* of the quest. As an artist, White sets himself the task of helping his readers work their ways through enveloping clouds of selfish ignorance and toward a stunning vision of sublime happiness; he knows all too well the price one pays for trying merely to survive, even for trying to be happy in an unhappy world, and so he will attempt to fashion an art that uses matter to transcend matter, aspiring to something like an absoluteness of spirit, a divine consciousness of self as pure spirit.

White is driven by his experience to contemplate the anomaly of man's unhappy existence in an order of nature which, other than for the presence of man, strikes one as harmonious and rational. Against the "economy of God's" natural creation (p. 433) man is a wasteful irrationality, for he behaves in mysterious ways for obscure reasons. In Essay No. 9 White attempts to explain the importance of recognizing that man's existence is a mystery when looked at against the background of a rational universe. In all the "order, beauty, and perfection" of the "great Architect's" stupendous creation, only man is disorderly, ugly, and imperfect. This is the view of the melancholy person, and so he is viewed by his fellows as a contemptible creature whose speculations are idle and unproductive. But, on the contrary, White assures his reader, the melancholy man, retired from the scenes of busy life, is the only one who can see the true condition of mankind: he sees the general condition as one of mystery amidst rational order, and he sees with keen sensitivity the plights of individuals whose sufferings testify to that mystery. The more one learns, from experience and reflection, the more serious and melancholy he becomes.

While all the rest of nature is happy in its lack of self-consciousness and in its tireless process of harmonious activity, mankind is a disturbing contradiction, attempting to be "natural" when his being is so "unnatural"—he merely aggravates his unhappiness so long as he attempts to be only natural. White speculates, in a conventional Christian way, that man's irrational unhappiness is the clearest possible sign of his having fallen from grace, of his having inherited the original sin of disobedience to God's will. The evidence of human unhappiness is the main argument of this essay (as though White's readers needed such evidence), and in presenting it White achieves the most concrete expression he ever does of his anguish and sympathy for his fellow creatures. He presents "a few detached scenes," including one of a beautiful woman who has lost her sexual innocence after being betrayed by her lover, another of a wretched family in which the husband and father marches off to join his regiment, leaving behind a poverty-stricken wife and children, and finally one of a young man pacing the courtyard of a prison where he is imprisoned for debt after having wasted an ample inheritance in a life of prodigality. All such signs of misery, marked by the melancholy man, are the offspring of vice, of failures to renounce the pursuit of worldly happiness in favor of constant self-sacrifice. The melancholy man must keep such scenes of vice ever before his reader's eyes as evidence of the inescapable irrationality of trying to be happy in an unhappy way. Nature's order and harmony are the circumstances, the frame, within which man's disorder and spiritual disharmony are made dramatic. The poet may, therefore, keep alive the scene of truth from which the priest can teach the necessary lesson for human happiness. Kirke White early realized that his urgency of vision was a call that combined a talent for poetry with a will to serve.

Enlightened service was to be Kirke White's chief objective as poet and priest. His reason would search for enlightenment, and his imagination would body forth the truths of his enlightenment. His program was clear to him, although his understanding was not yet strong and his tools of communication not yet mastered. He knew, however, that he could make progress in his personal development only if he penetrated the mysteries of all branches of knowledge still obscure to him. He had faith, nevertheless, that those particular mysteries of natural and social science were functions only of his own ignorance and that they could be cleared away by patient study. At the heart may be a religious, a spiritual, or moral mystery never to be understood, only to be imagined, but White did not shirk the task of attempting to get at the heart even of this mystery. When he surveys, as he does in Essay No. 11, the "progress of knowledge," he takes heart in his hopes that the most important truths can be discovered by the philosophic habit of mind he calls "melancholy."

Throughout these essays of his adolescence, Kirke White illustrates in practice what he advocated in principle: that withdrawal from the busy anxieties of worldly preoccupation could allow for an activity of thought and imagination that might lead to vision. Thus these "solitary effusions to the public" explore with, for such a young man, boldness and conviction the areas of most significance for White: first, the nature of the imagination itself, a power of vision that produces the very melancholy whose presence makes the mind aware of itself to itself; second, the modes and kinds of activity which sons of genius, those in the service of melancholy, pursue to fulfill their destinies; third, the special mode of poetry, as a valuable tool of civilization, for expressing the melancholy vision in modern times; finally, the field of philosophy, as White understood it, through which the melancholy man must range to understand himself, his fellow man, and the real nature of his calling to serve as well as to lead.

CHAPTER 3

In the Picturesque Tradition: Poetry for the Eye

IN his first version of *The Pleasures of Imagination,* Mark Akenside wrote that Fancy, "not content / With every food of life to nourish man," makes "all Nature beauty to his eye, / Or music to his ear" (III, 489-90; 492-93; p. 183).¹ Later, in his second version (which he worked on until his death in 1770), Akenside adds a fourth book in order to distinguish the man of genius, the poet, from all other men who know the "pleasures of the imagination." In the later poem, Akenside wishes to show how the poet can present, more successfully than any other artist, the same pleasures that Nature does herself; indeed, for the poet there are no natural limits on the range of his imagination: "A field is open'd wide as Nature's sphere; / Nay, wider; various as the sudden acts / Of human wit, and vast as the demands / Of human will" (IV, 105-108; p. 273). The poet makes available all the pleasures of nature as a function of his imagination: "To eyes, to ears, / To every organ of the copious mind, / He offereth all its treasures" (IV, 109-11; p. 273). Nature herself displays charms for all to take pleasure in, but the poet alone can present Nature's charms made subordinate to "human wit" and "human will." The emphasis of the earlier version is upon the ways imagination has to discover God in the works of Nature (III, 629-33; p. 187); however, the emphasis in the later version is upon "the copious mind" of man himself, unlimited by the natural boundaries of time and space.

Behind Akenside's poem lay ideas of art which were to become enormously influential throughout the eighteenth century in England. Those were ideas early formulated by Joseph Addison in certain of his *Spectator* papers and by the third Earl of Shaftesbury in *Characteristics*. Akenside acknowledges his debt to Addison in the preface to his first version of the poem: "These properties [about which the imagination is conversant] Mr. Addison had reduced to the three general classes of greatness, novelty, and beauty" (p. 116). In the poem itself Akenside says that "different minds / Incline to different objects":

> one pursues
> The vast alone, the wonderful, the wild:
> Another sighs for harmony and grace,
> And gentlest beauty. (III, 546-50; p. 185)

Between Addison's famous classes of "greatness, novelty, and beauty" and Akenside's "vast," "wild," and "beauty" there is of course much similarity, if not identity. A great many poets and aestheticians throughout the century pondered, debated, and defined over and over again what these terms meant; from Addison and Shaftesbury, through Akenside, Burke, and Hume, to Richard Payne Knight, there would be a continuous discussion.[2] Until William Gilpin in 1792 and Sir Uvedale Price in 1794, the dominant aesthetic terms for classifying the arts (or, rather, the "pleasures of the imagination") were "the beautiful" and "the sublime." Gilpin and Price added an important third term, "the picturesque," which "corrects the languor of beauty or the tension of sublimity."[3]

Henry Kirke White inherited these terms as a part of his intellectual and aesthetic baggage. His poetry can be divided into those kinds which aim for each of three effects, the sublime, the beautiful, and the picturesque; these are "the haunts of melancholy," as Eleanor M. Sickels describes the "three sorts" of poetry common to writers of the period.[4] The first is an effect of "greatness" (Addison) and "the vast alone" (Akenside), possible only for "the copious mind" of man (Akenside). The beautiful is an effect of "harmony and grace" (Akenside); and the picture--sque is an effect of "novelty" (Addison), "the wonderful, the wild" (Akenside). White's poems make their appeals for these effects, then, to particular modes of perception. He makes, again in the words of Akenside, "all Nature beauty to his eye" in the picturesque tradition; he makes Nature "music to his ear" in the tradition of the beautiful; and "to every organ of the copious mind" he offers all his poetic treasures in the tradition of the sublime.

I *"Clifton Grove": The Ravished Sight*

"Clifton Grove: A Sketch in Verse" is the title poem for Kirke White's only volume of poetry published during his lifetime, in 1803 (pp. 1-16).[5] The poem is a meditative description of a kind common to eighteenth-century literature, topographical in content and pedestrian (literally) in structure; it is composed in 492 lines of rhyming couplets, mixing description of the landscape with a tragic tale of romantic love associated with the region. It is sufficiently a part of the topographical tradition of the period that Robert Aubin takes note of it in his classic study of the genre.[6] White obviously labored over this poem, considering it his major work, and well might he have hoped it would win him the attention he desired, for it was a popular genre, mixing as it does the general with the particular, the conventional with the personal, and natural description with sentimental narrative. This poem is his experiment with "the theory of composition in the late eighteenth century [that] encourages above all pictorial representation and the dramatic expression, or display, of feeling."[7] The picturesque features of the poem are forecast by the subtitle, "a sketch in verse," promising that the reader will be able to see and hear with the narrator as he takes an evening stroll through Clifton Grove, as the poet presents his "well-composed picture, with suitably varied and harmonized form, colors, and lights," thus satisfying one of the meanings the term *picturesque* had for his contemporaries.[8] Readers of poetry from Milton to Collins to Cowper will correctly anticipate the visual imagery which the eighteenth century's critics and poets believed "was essential to effective poetry," as Patricia Meyer Spacks has noted. She goes on to say that "distinct visual imagery was almost a defining characteristic of successful poetry in most genres."[9] Because White is trying seriously to learn his craft by imitation, his readers will not be disappointed in thir anticipation.

The poem opens with images of the setting sun, evening sights and sounds, that make the time special for imagination. Sounds diminish and scenes soften, so that the usually unnoticed tinkle of a sheep-bell can now be heard even from "the distant vale," and its tinkle has the sound of "wild music." This is the time of the day when rustic laborers retire to their warm hearths to tell familiar stories, when urban mechanics, "pale" from their long hours of enclosed labor, rush out to enjoy a few hours of freedom, albeit a few hours of "customary sin." Evening is, then, special for all mankind, whether rustic or urban, as well as for the rest of nature; however, nature seems to rest in the fading light, while mankind merely redirects his movement, now less under restraint than during the daylight hours. The speaker himself finds the evening a special occasion for freedom, to ramble, speculate, and imagine. His favorite retreat is in Clifton Grove, where he comes "to pass the meditative hour" with invocations to a "sacred Power" that can inspire his vision and enliven his fancy; he hopes for the blessing of a "ravished sight," to be enrapt by the power of the grove, so translated in mind that he may detect "soft visions" and "mystic harmony" amidst or underlying the common scenes of harsh and confused reality, daylight scenes and mechanical reality. In Clifton Grove clouds can become the "giant shapes" of Ossian's narratives, and "hosts of sylphids" can sail "on the moonbeam."

The common scene is enchanted by the special forces of evening, becoming for the poet a metaphor of visionary activity, illustrating the point that "the picturesque mode was simply a mechanism for ordering the *mind's* impressions."[10] His emphasis is upon things of sight, radically transformed by the "ravished" vision. White flirts with the daemonic, a power that not only transforms objects of ordinary vision but also threatens constantly to dislocate the order we call ordinary and disorient the mind of the perceiver possessed by the daemon.

The speaker seems to be moving more deeply into the darkening woods by the third verse paragraph (line 49), into a region "where meeting trees create eternal night." One ray of light makes its way through the gloom, reflected "from yonder stream," and seeing it thus, the poet recalls scenes of a similar kind, or rather feelings of the same kind, from his childhood — when he was "a visionary boy." In such passages as this (ll. 49-72) White betrays his reading of Akenside and Beattie, although for most readers today such a passage will bear a striking resemblance to Wordsworth (and, indeed, White may have read such poems as "An Evening Walk," *Descriptive*

Sketches, and "Tintern Abbey"). As a child, the poet experienced the terrors of storms "with secret joy" and "awful pleasures big"—on this very spot where now he stands he was enlivened by the thunder and lightning of nature's power, and that childhood wildness of vision possesses him even amidst such calm beauty of the evening as he now observes. White suggests in such a passage that his speaker now observes with an "altered mind," in contrast with the mild scene surrounding him; the nature of the alteration is comparable with the childhood experience of terror and joy in the face of thunderstorms. The poem moves along a narrow edge between the calm of the present scene and the storm of childhood's past, as we alternate between the scenes from section to section.

The poet welcomes the peace of this "congenial" place as a retreat, then, not only from the frenzy of ordinary life but also from the passions of his childhood. Like the poem, the speaker alternates between relief at mature calm and exhausted childhood, and welcome recall of childhood passion and joyful frenzy. As he pursues his path through Clifton Grove, leaving behind the dark, enclosed space where the trees "create eternal night," he approaches a scene "where wide the prospect grows." It is a conventional way to block out space in his picturesque poem, to move from the constricted, dark area out, in a burst, to a prospect of wide dimensions—a chiaroscuro technique, but also a metaphor of growth, with a hint of birth. This movement between darkness and light is one of the typical characteristics of the picturesque, a certain "roughness and sudden variation, joined to irregularity."[11] The poet says that "a livelier light upon [his] vision flows" (l. 92) when he looks upon the growing prospect; the new scene is paradisal, with "hanging woods," moonlit flowers ("knot of bluebells" and "beds of violets"), and a nocturnal breeze loaded with fragrance. Such a scene of loveliness and life makes the poet lament the plight of mankind, that such natural virtue should so often be denied in favor of "Vice's deadly charms" (l. 107). This thought, occasioned by contrast, marks yet another alternation in the poem's structure; the verse paragraph beginning at line 103 explores the den of vice where many men have chosen to exist when they might, through a kind of natural piety, choose to inhabit such a valley as the one now visited by the poet in Clifton Grove.

White pictures Vice and Pleasure as wanton strumpets who

lure men from the healthy life of natural virtue. Clearly, vice is a matter of sexual license and virtue of sexual restraint, if not abstinence; however, Nature is itself so promising a "treasure" that White cannot ignore sexual pleasure as a virtue, which it can be if it is not an end in itself and experienced in the process of serving the greater end of procreation. The poet finds it difficult to believe that if all men but knew the "harmless pleasures of a harmless life," they would never again "pant for joys impure." His picture of Clifton Grove, with its "varied charms" and unvarying "sweets," should perform the ethical function of rescuing fallen creatures from strife-filled lives of "vile enjoyments." His own relationship with "fair Nature" is typically a love-relationship in which he would find in Nature a constancy and fidelity that he desires from his human relationships. Nature will be his lover whose "opening beauties" he will "enjoy . . . with a lover's eye" (ll. 125-26). These scenes of Clifton Grove are presented, therefore, "with a lover's eye," by one with "ravished sight." At this point in the poem, the adolescent yearning and imaginative displacement become too obvious for artful presentation, but the poem continues, struggling to define itself more clearly as the speaker moves ahead, perhaps awakening to some clearer goal than at first he had when he began his evening rambles.

What that goal may be is, however, still unclear to the reader in the passage beginning at line 127, where the poet celebrates his discovery that nature amply compensates the poor man with her treasures of beauty for the eye and ear, treasures more fully displayed for the person with a contented mind: "Content can soothe where'er by fortune placed" (l. 141). At this point in his rambles, the poet rests to survey the large scene into which he has recently burst. What he observes is an abundance of beauty, spread out as though poured forth from a great cornucopia. In a long passage beginning at line 151, he recapitulates the scene that opened the poem by describing the household where now the cottager has gone to sleep. It is late enough in the evening that if one is awakened from his sleep by the sounding of the church bell, he will be startled, frightened at such a "monitory toll." Even as he says so, the poet feels admonished to recommence his ramble: "A little onward let me bend my way" (l. 169), he tells himself in words that echo the opening line of *Samson Agonistes*. White's speaker is no Samson, but his situation is remotely, or metaphorically, like that of the blinded hero of the Bible, for both need to recover the vision that redeems, the power that liberates. Samson found his in God, while White's speaker must search through Nature for the "sacred Power."

He rouses himself from his easy posture, he strikes out for a particular "spot," anticipating some special delight associated with it, and then explains that he had as a youth spent many an hour "in visionary schemes" indulged while reclining there. If he did so then, why not now? Time usually destroys the hopes of youth, but for a favored few, himself perhaps one of them, time's erosion has no effect; "some can rise superior to the pain, / And in their breasts the charmer Hope retain" (ll. 195-96). He will make his way to that spot, and there he may discover if indeed he is one of the favored. His is to be a quest for that power all artists require to sanction their lives, a power variously called divine, imaginative, rational, or natural. In his essays, White called it "melancholy," although in this poem he does not. Many of the conditions are the same for discovering the virtues of melancholy in this poem as they were in the essays, and many of the same frustrations appear, but in the poem White makes stronger associations between external nature, memory, and melancholy (or imaginative vision) than he had in the essays.

He is having difficulty trying to accomplish what his contemporaries in the Romantic Movement will accomplish: externalizing in artful ways a process of creative imagination that is fundamentally internal. His basic structural metaphor, the nighttime ramble through a forest grove, is conventional enough, but he wants to do more than moralize on external scenes or paint them as picturesque scenes to please the eye of fancy. If White could do what he needed, he would explore his own mind—not Clifton Grove. White's real subject, as it was for most poets and aestheticians of the period, is psychological.

But Clifton Grove is where he must be, and there he makes his way the best he can. He winds his way "down the steep cliff," walks along "the margin of the solemn flood" of the river Trent, and turns to look around at this new scene, or rather from this new perspective. He discovers what he has been searching for, the sacred spot, a place of mind as well as a spot of earth. White tries here to express the same strange vision of harmony that Wordsworth was writing about (at about the same time) when he crossed the Simplon Pass. White's way of putting it, though not so successful as Wordsworth's, begins at line 221:

> Above, below, where'er I turn my eyes,
> Rocks, waters, woods, in grand succession rise.
> High up the cliff the varied groves ascend,
> And mournful larches o'er the wave impend.
> Around, what sounds, what magic sounds arise,
> What glimmering scenes salute my ravished eyes!

The passage continues for another twelve lines, expressing the awe of the mind in the presence of some greater power, on the threshold of discovering some great key to understanding the spiritual significance of this sensuous existence. Tactfully, White does not attempt to pass over the threshold, or even, like Wordsworth, to explain in language of abstract philosophy what the spiritual significance might be. Instead, he tells a story.

At this point we may feel that the poem breaks apart, fastening in mechanical fashion a narrative onto a descriptive piece. But White's intent is clear: he wishes to explain that the scene just celebrated derives its power, if not its significance, from a function of the mind, a function we would not hesitate to call imagination although the young poet not fully educated by the mature poetry of Wordsworth might understandably have to grope for a name for this power (indeed, Wordsworth had trouble naming the power). The spot of nature is, then, special because it has received a stamp of the human mind, a stamp that this journey is designed to uncover for us. "In this sequestered spot, when youth / Gave to each tale the holy force of truth" (ll. 239-40), the poet had lingered when he was young, hearing a tale sung by a milkmaid, a tale that rang throughout the woodland and still rings for the enlivened sensibility. It is a tale of "beauteous Margaret" and her lover, "Bateman." They lived over a hundred years ago, but the force of their lives remains as a haunting presence in this special place in Clifton Grove.

In this very spot to which we have been led, Margaret and Bateman made love with one another and exchanged sacred vows of fidelity. Nature was a witness to their love, and still yet the trees bear "mementos of the fated pair." We know their lives were to be unhappy because the "mementos" are a "blasted yew" and a "mouldering walnut bare." White's poem now seeks to penetrate the mystery of the scene, to find and show what happened to mark this spot in such a way. The story is simple: Bateman meets Margaret in their customary place, but she has come there long before he arrives, and she is apprehensive. He tells her that he must leave England, travel far away for three years "to languish in a foreign land," and he tells her of his fears that Margaret will forget him while he is gone. She promises always to be faithful, making her vow on threat of punishment by "fiends of hell" should she break it:

> "Hear me, just God! if from my traitorous heart
> My Bateman's fond remembrance e'er shall part,
> If, when he hail again his native shore,
> He finds his Margaret true to him no more,
> May fiends of hell, and every power of dread,
> Conjoined, then drag me from my perjured bed,
> And hurl me headlong down these awful steeps,
> To find deserved death in yonder deeps!" (ll. 325-32)

Under such circumstances, the lovers part, although Bateman still felt "melancholy bodings." After two years of separation, Margaret indeed betrayed her vow to Bateman, married a man who "offered wealth, and all the joys of life." When Bateman returned, six months after the marriage, he drowned himself in the river by the very spot where they had made love in happier days. Margaret was pregnant, and so her life was prolonged to allow the birth of the child. But on the evening of the birth, something mysterious and terrible happened; friends and kinsmen surrounded Margaret's bed to protect her from danger, but they fell asleep and Margaret disappeared before daybreak, "And never more the weeping train were doomed / To view the false one, in the deeps intombed." Witnesses tell of hideous screams they heard during the night of Margaret's disappearance, and to this day natives can show one the spot where she was pulled down to her death by the demons—in the same watery grave where Bateman drowned himself.

The spot is made sacred, then, by powers of death, birth, and demons. Its force is a combination of natural and supernatural power working to enforce moral laws of love, fidelity, and revenge. The beauty of the place is, for White, a function of natural forms illuminated by human passion; it is a place of "melancholy power" that gives "a romantic cadence" to all sights and sounds (ll. 445, 454). Even when he cannot journey back to this sacred spot, wherever his "devious track" may lead, the poet can travel here by the strength of memory. Like Wordsworth, White celebrates the importance of memory for recovering imaginative strength, and also like Wordsworth, he attaches great value to "spots of time" which he can visit as sacred shrines to his youthful vitality.

But White's poem is not accomplished in the Wordsworthian manner. Instead, he has chosen to form it according to more "classical" principles, imitating the closed couplet form of the Augustans (and more recently, Johnson, Goldsmith, and Crabbe). White uses the devices of alliteration ("To find *d*eserved *d*eath in yonder *d*eeps"), assonance ("The m*ai*den w*ai*ted *a*t the *a*ccustomed bower"), end-stopped lines, masculine rhymes, and medial caesuras (with variations). But his most important device is grammatical, using adverbs of time and place and verbal imperatives to give directions to the reader as a guide through the region, where he points out the various "scenes" to view:

> Lo! in the west fast fades the lingering light. (l. 1)
> Now, when the rustic wears the social smile. . . . (l. 15)
> Now, now, my solitary way I bend. . . . (l. 25)
> Here lonely wandering o'er the sylvan bower,
> I come to pass the meditative hour. (ll. 29-30)
> Behind me, lo! the peaceful hamlet lies. (l. 151)

Throughout the poem, he employs these verbal signs to control the movement of the speaker-reader across the picturesque landscape. The importance of sight is emphasized by verbs of looking, seeing, and observing; and the images of vision are numerous (as are images of hearing). White employs personification to render intellectual significance from his scenic landscapes: "'Twas here, when Hope, presiding o'er my breast, / In vivid colours every prospect dressed" (l. 177-78).

While he is sincerely attempting to present the experience of rambling through the grove as if it were an exploration of his past and of his mind, to discover the sources of his imaginative strength, White is hampered by his models of imitation, especially such poems as Thomas Warton's "Pleasures of

Melancholy," Joseph Warton's "The Enthusiast," and even Oliver Goldsmith's "The Traveler." White is, however, in his apprenticeship and his exercises in imitation are necessary first steps for his stylistic growth, as all artists must discover; he was "born too late to have felt the personal influence of the Wartons, and yet" as Eleanor Sickels has noted, he is "to be counted among their followers." But, she goes on to add, he "was perhaps the most original and promising, as he was certainly the most introspective and romantic, of them all."[12] Like his Romantic contemporaries, White does not limit himself to imitations of the Augustans' favorite form; he explores all kinds and models, including songs, sonnets, ballads, odes, blank verse, drama, and Spenserian stanzas.

II Songs and Sonnets: The Tear-Filled Eye

Not all White's songs and sonnets are constructed to emphasize the experience of seeing and vision, but enough are to suggest that he composed them in a way that relies upon conventions of the picturesque tradition. One striking feature that recurs in many of these poems is the image of the "tear-filled eye," expressing not only the sentimentality of uncontrollable emotion, of sadness and grief, of melancholy and nostalgia, but also the mystery of existence as, in Virgil's phrase, "tears in the nature of things."[13] The interesting thing about White's use of this image is the way the poet relies upon it to condition vision, to spread, as it were, a film or haze of obscurity across the field of sight and so render it strange, even mysterious, but certainly more malleable to the pressure of imagination. While we might be inclined to say that White is merely exploiting a popular convention of sentimentality, we can nevertheless entertain as a possibility his more conscious artistic use of the popular figure of speech.

The eye proves to be too passive an organ of imagination for White, whose lyrics work upon the matter of vision to translate into the form of song. Most of his successful poems struggle against the forms of natural matter, presented as scenes in a picturesque view, to reorganize or translate into less rigid forms of sound, aiming, as we shall see later, to raise even sound into the domain of thought, where form is absolute and unconditioned by nature's body. His fragmentary poem, beginning "Ah! who can say" (p. 99), turns from a "fair . . . view" and "sad scenes" to scan "the illusive past and dark futurity" "with thoughtful eye." This fragment aptly illustrates the main tendency of White's verse: to sublimate vision by way of the "thoughtful eye," with perhaps sound, shaped as music, serving in a mediating way. In his finished sonnet "To the Moon" (p. 183), White hails the appearance of a November moon as it emerges "from the misty verge / Of the horizon dim" to the accompaniment of "the year's funereal dirge" made by the wind as it sweeps through "the leafless grove." Natural music serves to interpret the meaning of the experience of vision.

"To the Moon" deserves further consideration as a fine example of White's forming a sonnet in the same tradition that his favorite sonneteer William Lisle Bowles had followed. White focuses upon the scene as visionary, nature in the process of revealing its mysteries:

> Sublime, emerging from the misty verge
>   Of the horizon dim, thee, Moon, I hail,
>   As, sweeping o'er the leafless grove, the gale
> Seems to repeat the year's funereal dirge.
> Now Autumn sickens on the languid sight,
>   And leaves bestrew the wanderer's lonely way,
> Now unto thee, pale arbitress of night,
>   With double joy my homage do I pay.
>   When clouds disguise the glories of the day,
> And stern November sheds her boisterous blight,
>   How doubly sweet to mark the moony ray
> Shoot through the mist from the ethereal height,
>   And, still unchanged, back to the memory bring
> The smiles Favonian of life's earliest spring!

The misty scene shot through with moonlight, the dirge made by the gale sweeping through the trees, the sternly denuded landscape—all are bare to the poet's eye. The season is appropriate for uncovering realities, but the presence of the mist renders that same bared reality ambiguously beneath the pale moonlight. White's poem celebrates not the picture of a November evening, but the *transformation* made possible by the special conditions of that evening; the poem is, like much of Thomson's poetry, more interested in "an action than a scene, an activity rather than nature."[14] In the sudden emergence of a heavenly light upon a naked landscape is a special metaphor of the revelatory imagination at work, although White's way of indicating this is to conclude with a somewhat lame association with remembrance of "life's earliest spring."

In nine of his short poems, four songs and five sonnets, White composes his picturesque scenes as "causes" for the tear-dimmed eyes of his speakers; these scenes range from a winter prospect for an orphan boy to a threatening storm at sea for a frightened sailor. In each situation, the speaker (or a person within the speaker's view) signals his sorrow with a tear filled eye. Usually the sorrow can be explained in terms of the picture we are invited to share with the speaker, but sometimes the wash of tears is inexplicable; the poems of sorrow from mysterious causes are generally the better of White's poems in this category. That is, the more subjective his statement, the more nearly he comes to probing the strange depths of feeling in the human subject and the more distant he grows from the external world of fixity and fact, the more authentic White's poetry becomes.

The more objective, and so more picturesque, poems include "The Wandering Boy," "Fanny! Upon Thy Breast," "The Unhappy Poet Dermody in a Storm," "By a Female Lunatic to a Lady"; those poems which retain the picturesque but center on the mysterious tear not explained by anything in the setting include "I'm Pleased, and Yet I'm Sad," "Solitude," "To a Taper," "Ye Unseen Spirits," and "To April." Those poems which seem most picturesque are the very ones which develop a special tension of mystery, when the tear dims an eye that should take pleasure from the scene it views. White is attempting to capture what better poets, such as Tennyson in "Tears, Idle Tears" and Keats in his "Ode on Melancholy," would later be able to render: the sorrow of all mortal beauty. While there is no obvious mystery surrounding the cause of the "chilling tear" that stands in the eye of "The Wandering Boy" (p. 209), the poet nevertheless chooses to render his speaker's pathetic condition in terms that point to a more profound condition than the social misery of the cold and outcast orphan who weeps out his song (somewhat like the boys of Blake's *Songs of Experience*). Nothing is capable of comforting the eye filled with a "chilling tear," for here is a vision metaphysically blurred, not simply pained by physical discomfort. The boy's very "heart . . . is cold as it beats in [his] breast," because, as we learn, he is without parents, and that is something that can never be compensated in this life; his cold heart and cold tears are calls to death, the only comfort he can hope for when his entire life is a winter world of keen wind and snowstorms. The boy sees what he is.

Separation from a loved one, suffered by the "wandering boy," is what "really" causes the "chilling tear" through which he views the wintry world of his existence. Similarly, in the sonnet "Fanny! Upon Thy Breast" (p. 94), the speaker feels a tear on his cheek when he turns around to look for his beloved and, not finding her, wonders if he was only dreaming when he saw her face, with a cold eye and bloodless lip. He felt her presence, he turned weeping to see her, but seeing her not, he imagines her in her "cold grave," where he will lie with her in his thoughts, "through the long wintry night." Like "The Wandering Boy," the speaker of this sonnet invests the world of his vision with the same cold he feels, a chilling effect of loneliness. In both poems, White projects the hope of reunion in death, although even that is imagined as occurring in a "dark house" where it is a cold and "long wintry night."

In a somewhat more successful poem, his sonnet "The Unhappy Poet Dermody in a Storm" (p. 178), White does not attempt to identify completely with his speaker. Instead, he sets up a scene on board a ship that seems doomed to sinking in the storm, where the pilot is saddened by his thought that he will soon be separated from his "wife, and little home, and chubby lad," so that a "half strangled tear bedews his eyes." The pilot is struggling manfully to keep his vision clear as he steers through the storm, and so he fights back the tears that cloud his sight: by contrast, the poet Dermody, also on board the tossing ship, has no dread, no fear or sorrow, and so no tears in his eyes. The man of responsible social action has an emotional investment that wrings tears from him at a critical moment; the artist looks with clear sight and without passion, but at the terrible price of having no loved ones to mourn him if he should die. This sonnet has a success that many of White's other poems lack because here is an irony of circumstance that allows the poem to speak by indirection rather than by expostulation and direct statement. When the poet Dermody dies, or so he imagines, "the wild winds will ring my funeral knell, / Sweetly as solemn peal of pious passing-bell." The tear may be in the pilot's eye, but the poet has the greater cause to weep.

In a similarly ironic fashion, the sonnet "By a Female Lunatic to a Lady" (p. 177) juxtaposes the weeping (and so sentimental) "lady" with the expostulating (but realistic) "maniac" who is the object of the lady's sorrow. This poem, with its otherwise "mean or unpleasant" subject, is picturesque in one of the usual senses that it forms a "pleasing picture" from unpleasant objects.[15] The speaker exclaims that the lady has no reason to weep, or at least no reasons at all like the maniac's own reasons, which include the deaths of her mother, her brother, and her lover. Yet she does not weep, wretched though her heart might be. And so she asks, either because she is insane and does not understand, or because she is profoundly sane and bitterly understands; "whence the tear which dims the lovely eye?" Contrasting her own hope for quiet peace with the lady's weeping, the maniac speaker tells the lady to go her way and "pluck the roses while they bloom." Like the speakers of the other poems we have been examining here, the maniac of this poem also imagines her only comfort in death, a place of "peaceful sleep" but not, as in the others, wintry and cold; instead, her death will lay her beneath "the green sod." But, then, she is a "lunatic," as White's title has told us.

No such ironies of circumstance operate in the next group of poems, more picturesque than the ones just examined but less dramatic and less objective nevertheless. In these songs and sonnets, set in scenes of natural landscape at different times of the day and in different seasons, the speakers claim to feel a pleasant satisfaction in their lives at the very moment they feel tears coming to their eyes. Something in themselves seems to protest their statements of satisfaction. In the song "I'm Pleased, and Yet I'm Sad" (p. 91), the poet even asserts that he is "to bliss . . . all alive." Sitting alone at twilight, he looks out his window and hears the bells toll out the time—five o'clock. He watches the silver clouds pass over the "blue hill's woody top" and he hears the sweet music from the bells fill the air. And while he feels "inly glad," the "tear-drop fills [his] eye." He claims that he does "not know why / Or wherefore [he is] sad."

This mixture of happiness and sorrow is a complex blend of emotions that White tries again and again to communicate. White allows his imagination the play of ambiguity and contradiction in this song that communicates perplexity in the speaker and mystery for the poem. We may rightly think that White captures in the poem a bit of the maturity he was himself realizing in his life, that life is not simple, nor clearly defined: he could, like his speaker, be happy and unhappy at the same moment. At the heart of his urgency to be, as fully as possible, is a constant anxiety that he may cease to be, utterly and forever. That anxiety is often admitted in terms of the poetry as a hope for release from life, as a yearning for stillness and silence in the grave: in personal terms, White's expression of hope for the peace of death is a defensive reaction to protect his strong desire for life and movement and growth from the pain of disappointment and despair.

Tension between his energy of life and pleasure in beauty, and his anxiety for death and wish for quiet darkness—this is the quality which underlies White's poem on "Solitude" (p. 93). It, like "I'm Pleased, and Yet I'm Sad," develops a pattern of perplexing emotion as the poet attempts to discover the cause for "the silent tear." He weeps because he is "all alone" in a world that teems with life and companionship for others; the "tired hedger hies him home," the "star looks on [the] breast" of a "woodland pool," and even the "autumn leaf . . . floats upon the water's bed." All things come to rest in sympathetic bosoms—except for the speaker, for whom nothing seems to sigh in sympathy. His loneliness is absolute and unconditioned, unlike anything else in nature. His weeping is a function of his spiritual alienation, something he can deal with as a matter of imagination:

> Yet in my dreams a form I view,
> That thinks on me, and loves me too;
> I start, and when the vision's flown,
> I weep that I am all alone.

A world of sympathy and love is the dream; his loneliness and weeping is the reality. A simplified reading of this poem would leave White open to the charge of sentimentality, but acknowledging even this little bit of complexity suggests that the poet has a fine capacity, at least, for aesthetic subtlety.

The sonnet "To a Taper" (p. 186) paints a conventional picture of the candle burning down while the poet meditates at the deep of midnight as the wind roars through a dark wood outside. The theme is again loneliness and, while he watches the taper burn slowly away with a light that grows dimmer and dimmer, the poet feels again "the sad meaning tear" come to his eye. Nature's darkness and wild, hostile environment are so uninviting that he protests he does not mind the prospect of death; his tear is not mixed "wth dread," for if death is like the dying of the candle's flame, then it is to be welcomed as a gentle fading away into quiet darkness. We are not entirely convinced that the speaker accepts his end so easily, however; he says that maybe his life will "fade in loneliness, unwept, away" just like the fading light of the candle, but notice that *he* is weeping while he watches the dying candle. Who, then, if the simile is to hold, will weep for him *as* he weeps for the candle? We notice also that he feels the tear come to his eye, not as he imagines the quiet fading of death, but rather when his "eye "eye surveys the solitary gloom" that surrounds him. In fact, he weeps because he protests against the fading of light and because the prospect of death is a threat of even greater solitude. The tear is a confession of the very "dread" he asserts he does not feel.

Two sonnets, "Ye Unseen Spirits" (p. 186) and "To April" (p. 185), exemplify further the ways White renders the objective picture of natural landscape as an occasion for subjective emotion. But, more than that, they illustrate the logical culmination of his increasing tendency to compose his poems according to a principle of tension—between the need to describe an external scene and an opposing urge to ignore or transform the external scene. "Unseen Spirits" testifies to the poet's urge to ignore environment, although it does rely upon sounds that "steal on the musing poet's pensive ear." The meaning of life, as well as the underlying meaning of "nature," can be discovered most easily when the resistant forms of sight are dissolved into the "unseen spirits" of sound. White, like Thomson, "retreats from reliance on the visual," as Patricia Spacks has noted; for both poets, "the sense of hearing becomes increasingly important."[16] What is seen may not account for "the full tear" so well as what is heard (as a number of poets have said, Wordsworth in "Tintern Abbey" and Arnold in "Dover Beach," for example). When nature refuses to yield up her visual forms to the power of sound, then the poet of imagination can transform all sight into vision until the scene becomes an "emblem of life," as in "To April." In this, the last poem of this section, White does the utmost he can with the landscape tradition: he makes out of the features of an April scene a set of emotional equivalents.

These are not exactly "objective correlatives," for White does

In the Picturesque Tradition: Poetry for the Eye 71

not attempt to set before us those things which cause us to feel the emotion he seeks to create; instead, they are subjective "personifications" of the great impersonal, the vast neutral terrain we call so easily "nature." When he invites us to "see changeful April sail / In varying vest along the shadowy skies," White asks us to participate in a well-established convention that realizes the importance of humanizing all nature, a convention made especially powerful for readers in White's time by such poets as James Thomson and William Collins. Personified abstraction was, according to Earl Wasserman, "considered the requisite means of conveying the higher forms of knowledge to the necessarily imperfect human understanding."[17] "Changeful" April is a very appropriate image for White to choose as his "emblem of life," for his theme of mutability and natural process could not better be pictured than by an April shower through which the sun shines. In this image nature's self expresses the complexity of sorrow mixed with joy, "smiling through the tear that dims her eyes."

White composed at least twenty-three sonnets. Remembering his call in Essay No. 5 of his *Melancholy Hours* for British poets to avoid competition with the Continental "jingles" called "sonnets," we might be surprised that White would compose a "quatorzain" at all. His sonnets are, despite his earlier aversion, often graceful and unforced, only occasionally marred by ungainly inversions of syntax to achieve the necessary rhymes. "Warton's espousal of the sonnet helped give it a new lease on life, and it proved to have resources beyond what anyone could have expected."[18] White, always ready to follow the Wartons, could not for long have resisted experimenting with the sonnet. He discovered the form to be as interesting and challenging as his Romantic contemporaries were finding for themselves, but he must also have been slightly embarrassed for having written his essay criticizing the sonnet as inappropriate for English poets. His patron, and sometime poet himself, Capel Lofft, remonstrated with White for having scoffed at the sonnet, and White, with good humor, wrote this sonnet, as a "Recantatory, in Reply to [Capel Lofft's] Elegant Admonition" (p. 180):

> Let the sublimer muse, who, wrapped in night,
> Rides on the raven pennons of the storm,
> Or o'er the field, with purple havoc warm,

> Lashes her steeds, and sings along the fight;
> Let her, whom more ferocious strains delight,
>   Disdain the plaintive sonnet's little form,
>   And scorn to its wild cadence to conform,
> The impetuous tenor of her hardy flight.
> But me, far lowliest of the sylvan train,
>   Who wake the wood-nymphs from the forest shade
>   With wildest song; me,—much behoves thy aid
> Of mingled melody, to grace my strain,
> And give it power to please, as soft it flows
> Through the smooth murmurs of thy frequent close.

When we realize that his most ambitious efforts in verse are poems which strive for the sublime effect that here he leaves for the "plaintive sonnet's little form," we better appreciate White's capacity for self-examination and even his sense of humor. He especially knows the value of tact and decorum, leaving the "ferocious strains" for sublime forms and the "smooth murmurs" for the songs and sonnets. These are the soft streams that flow through his more ambitious forest of dark and mighty forms.

III *"Ode to H. Fuseli": The Genius of Vision*

One of White's most ambitious poems is his ode composed as a tribute to the art of Henry Fuseli (pp. 139–42), whose engravings White had seen and admired for their power to inspire horror and awe. The allusions in the poem suggest that White had seen not only an engraving of Fuseli's most famous painting, *The Nightmare,* but also his illustrations for Dante's *Divine Comedy* and perhaps those he did for *The Nibelungenlied,* Wieland's *Oberon,* and Cowper's *The Task* (although these last may have appeared too late for White to have seen).[19] Fuseli's drawings were simply fine examples for White of the power of vision, of sight, to excite imagination and charge emotion. His ode is an intricately designed, complexly conceived poem in the tradition of the irregular Pindaric.

It is made of five stanzas of varying length (28 lines, 12 lines, 48 lines, 4 lines, and 10 lines), and lines that vary between the pentameter and the octosyllabic; the pentameters occur in quatrains rhyming *abba* (there is one exception in the third stanza, where the rhyme is *abab*) and the octosyllabic lines occur in rhyming couplets, which make up the main body of the poem. The first three stanzas open with quatrains, the fourth stanza has no quatrains, and the final stanza concludes with a quatrain. White used the quatrain, then, as a kind of motif for developing his themes and also as a device for framing the poem as a whole. Within the quatrains are couplet rhymes that will be picked up by the main body of each stanza, and so as a musical device the quatrain introduces sounds that are picked up and repeated throughout the poem. In addition, the couplet rhymes within the quatrains produce a play of imagery that develops the important visual experience of contrast between height and depth: "deep" / "sleep"; "deep" / "creep"; "deep" / "sleep"; "steep" / "sleep." Since the direction of the poem is from heights to depths, as the power of genius descends and ascends to bless the artist, these rhymes perform important functions of composition and theme.

Overall, the poem's subject is divided into three parts. The first part (stanzas 1-2) calls upon the "genius of horror and romantic awe" as a "mighty magician" to reveal who will inherit the power once possessed by the poet Dante; in this first part, the first stanza describes the sources of the power in, first, its guise of "horror" and, second, of "romantic awe," feelings which the poet would want to understand, being a follower of "the Gray-Warton-Collins group" that encouraged writers in a "school [of] enthusiasts for the Gothic and the picturesque."[20] Then it asks the critical question, critical because the structure and meaning of the poem turn upon the answer, at lines 33-36. As a power of horror, the genius of vision lives amidst lightning pierced storms and darkness where it listens for the "death-shrieks" of drowning mariners; as a power of romantic awe, it lives in clear and calm regions of such harmony that even the breeze sounds like music. This genius, nourished by such scenes of horror and romance, "fill'st the mind" "with mighty visions" such as Dante once experienced. An important function of such power, as exemplified by Dante, is its ability to break through the barriers of darkness and evil to reveal, or expose, them to the clear light of day and human reason. White, however, does not particularly celebrate the didactic function of such revelatory power; instead, he praises the power itself, as a capacity for discovering and asserting a realm of human being suppressed or kept secret from ordinary consciousness.

The second part (stanzas 3-4) supplies the answer to the question, who will inherit the power of visionary genius? The magic wand has been discovered again, in the grasp of Henry Fuseli, the "mighty magician" of the new age: "He throws thy dark-wrought tunic on, / Fuesslin waves thy wand" (ll. 46-47). He is able to raise images that have long been dormant, buried for long ages beneath darkness and ignorance. Fuseli has the power to astonish us with horror and romantic awe because he is a son of genius, nurtured by the same scenes and forces which once nurtured the poet Dante. Most of the third stanza describes the education of Fuseli as a son of the "mighty magician." His training repeats the form which White outlined in stanza one to describe the sources of horror and romantic awe; that is, his training will be a repetition of the same experiences which all visionary artists undergo, including, we may think, White himself. This training in horror and awe is administered by Superstition (ll. 61-74), Pity (ll. 75-88), and finally, Taste (ll. 89-92).

Superstition is an important servant of visionary genius, for she forces a separation from the narrow bonds of the ordinary, of the common, and the rational. The ability to "suspend disbelief for the moment" (as Coleridge said) is necessary for the training of the visionary artist, and Superstition is a useful instructor in the discovery of that ability. Pity's task is to humanize the material of vision, to assure a sympathy with the plight of suffering mankind, so that one's "negative capability" (to use Keats's phrase) not become the cause of one's dehumanization. Finally, Taste, which receives a stanza to itself, teaches the novice the importance of "polish" and unity through form. Taste will assure that the vision has the boundaries that will make its communication possible as art rather than as accident: "Glowing with wild, yet chastened heat, / The wondrous work is now complete" (ll. 91-92)

Throughout this section the key term is conveyed by words of sight or looking. As in "Clifton Grove" we are invited to share with the poet an experience of ravishment, as our vision is entertained along with the instruction of the novice artist until it may seize with confidence upon "the visionary spear," a tool (weapon, in fact) of the imagination, useful for producing personifications; this it can do best "when the rational mind is laid asleep, as in visions."[21] White puns upon the magician's wand as an artist's pencil (whether the artist is poet or painter) and then as a visionary spear that strikes through rational defenses and defends against the bluntness of the common. We are to see "the savage feast and spectred fight" in Odin's Hall; we are to feel with pity as we hear the sighs of troubled spirits and see the "gliding sprite" as it moves through the Fancy. Again, however, White is less concerned to recreate the scenes of vision than he is to celebrate the *power* that can show forth such visions; for him, as for William Cowper, according to Patricia Spacks, "the seeing itself implied the transcendental truth; the physical power of vision had become a spiritual reality."[22] He is more likely to render a thought or a thing visible by means of an epithet than by a listing or positioning of objects: for example, *"sullen* tempests," *"caverned* dell," and *"silent beam* of night." [23] White's "pictures" are firmly within the convention of allegory through personification, a poetic device which White knew could provide his readers with "a very special sort of delight. . . . It lends strangeness to the conventional; it brings the dead to life," as Bertrand Bronson has argued.[24] While that delight in the personification may have reached its peak in the mid-eighteenth century, according to Bronson, the expectation by readers continued well into White's lifetime (so much so that Wordsworth made it a major point of attack in the celebrated Preface to his *Lyrical Ballads*). The convention of allegory through personification was made very popular in White's time by the achievements of poets such as Gray and Collins (whose own "Ode on the Poetical Character" may have supplied White with an excellent model for this ode "To H. Fuseli").

The third, and last, part of the poem (stanza 5) is a comparison (and contrast) between the Poet and the Painter, both of whom have access to the visionary power of this genius that inspires horror and romantic awe. White is most struck by the dramatic force and permanence of the painter's art:

> The Poet dreams:—the shadow flies,
> And fainting fast its image dies.
> But lo! the Painter's magic force
> Arrests the phantom's fleeting course;
> It lives—it lives—the canvass glows,
> And tenfold vigour o'er it flows.
> The Bard beholds the work achieved,
>   And as he sees the shadow rise
>   Sublime before his wondering eyes,
> Starts at the image his own mind conceived. (ll. 92-102)

Both the poet and the painter are nourished by the same genius, both draw upon the same power, and both render in material forms the matter of mind. Although White's tribute to the painter's art is a fine compliment, his poem itself has the last word, a word that can articulate mind in clearer ways than either painting or music. Indeed, painting and the picturesque constitute the most elementary if fundamental form of the aesthetic experience. As White realizes, by instinct if not always by reason, art should conduct one from matter to spirit, from fact to fancy, from sense to idea, without dividing either from the other in a kind of ladder of ascent represented by the arts of painting, music, and poetry.

CHAPTER 4

In the Tradition of the Beautiful: Poetry for the Ear

IN the opening stanza of his "Ode to Simplicity," William Collins addresses "simplicity" this way:

> O thou by Nature taught
> To breathe her genuine thought,
> In numbers warmly pure and sweetly strong:
> Who first on mountains wild
> In Fancy, liveliest child,
> Thy babe or Pleasure's, nursed the powers of song![1]

It was Simplicity that inspired classical Greek poetry, that "soothed sweetly sad Electra's poet's ear" (l. 18), and Collins hopes for a similar inspiration for himself:

> O sister meek of Truth,
> To my admiring youth
> Thy sober aid and native charms infuse!
> The flowers that sweetest breathe,
> Though Beauty culled the wreath,
> Still ask thy hand to range their ordered hues. (ll. 25-30)

In these two stanzas, Collins has stated several principles of aesthetics which were important to a great many English poets of the eighteenth century, including Kirke White (whose poetry shows evidence of considerable influence from Collins and Collins's friend Joseph Warton).[2]

These principles are that *simplicity* is the pupil of nature, the sister of truth, and, somewhat surprisingly, the mother of fancy. When Collins says that Fancy is "thy babe or Pleasure's," he is either suggesting that fancy is a product of the marriage between simplicity and pleasure, or that fancy is the child of one or the other, but of which one is uncertain. Some doubt about which is the parent of fancy adds some richness to the poem, but a resolution of the question does not affect the main point: that fancy derives from simplicity, and that "the powers of song" are nursed in fancy by simplicity. Complementing its powers of song is simplicity's power of arrangement: "Though Beauty culled the wreath, / Still ask thy hand to range their ordered hues." Truth is not Beauty, then, Keats's Urn to the contrary notwithstanding, until it has been joined by its sister Simplicity in a process of selection ("culled") and arrangement ("to range") toward the end of a new order ("their ordered hues").

Collins's poem deplores the decline of simplicity's powers throughout the history of poetry since the Greeks, and his main theme in this ode as in so much of his poetry, is an appeal for the return of poetic power for himself and his time. This "artist's struggle with his vocation," as Geoffrey Hartman has described it, "with past masters and the 'pastness' of art in modern society—seems to be a version of a universal human struggle: of genius with Genius, and of genius with genius loci (spirit of place)."[3] Collins's poetry characteristically has a tone of anxiety that derives from this "struggle," an anxiety that Harold Bloom, says is Collins's fear of his "own daemon"[4] and that Thomas Weiskel elaborated to show that the sublime is a "kind of homeopathic therapy" for various anxieties afflicting writers throughout the eighteenth century.[5] Much of Kirke White's poetry betrays a comparable anxiety for himself and his time, although he does not often make it a main theme of his writing. He does, however, benefit from insights like these in Collins's ode so that we may consider a large group of White's poetry in the tradition of music as the dominant art of the beautiful.

In this tradition poetry invoked the powers of music to move human passions as in the ancient times it was wont to do, to move thought and feeling into an harmonious unity of natural pleasure "that flows from divine Order." This "Newton had demonstrated," Earl Wasserman explains, "and the Shaftesburians had argued that Harmony in its different forms is Beauty and Moral Goodness."[6] Music, and poetry as music have a "native simple heart, / Devote[d] to Virtue, fancy, art" (as in Collins's "ode for music," "The Passions," ll. 103-104).

Edmund Burke would agree with Collins that simplicity's

powers of song in the service of beauty produce sweet harmonies. In his *Philosophical Enquiry into the Origin of Our Ideas of the Sublime and Beautiful* (which Kirke White read),[7] Burke cites a passage from Milton's "L'Allegro" to illustrate "how far sweet or beautiful sounds agree with our descriptions of beauty in other senses," and what he finds typical in Milton's celebration of music is its "softness, the winding surface, the unbroken continuance, the easy gradation" that characterizes "the beautiful in other things."[8] These important attributes, signalled in Milton's poem by such terms as "soft Lydian airs," "linked sweetness," "melting voice," and "the hidden soul of harmony," are similar to "the qualities of beauty" that Burke lists in his "Recapitulation" of Part III:

On the whole, the qualities of beauty, as they are merely sensible qualities, are the following. First to be comparatively small. Secondly, to be smooth. Thirdly, to have a variety in the direction of the parts; but fourthly, to have those parts not angular, but melted as it were into each other. Fifthly, to be of a delicate frame, without any remarkable appearance of strength. Sixthly, to have its colours clear and bright; but not strong and glaring. Seventhly, or if it should have any glaring colour, to have it diversified with others. (p. 117)

Burke does not say that music is the only art of the beautiful; however, music as an art of sound is better able to create the experience of sweet and soft harmony than is the picturesque, because sound seems to be a more fluid (active) medium than sight (passive). Music also makes a more successful appeal to that emotion which Burke argues is fundamental to the experience of the beautiful: love. He is careful to distinguish it from "desire or lust":

By beauty I mean, that quality or those qualities in bodies by which they cause love, or some passion similar to it. . . . I likewise distinguish love, by which I mean that satisfaction which arises to the mind upon contemplating anything beautiful, of whatsoever nature it may be, from desire or lust; which is an energy of the mind, that hurries us on to the possession of certain objects, that do not affect us as they are beautiful, but by means altogether different. (p. 91)

While neither Collins nor White may exactly agree with Burke on this point, both poets frequently describe sights and sounds as if they were attributes of a woman whose beauty moves them to feelings of "love."

I Songs and Ballads: The Frozen Ear

Many of White's poems are lyrics that sing the power of music to soothe, lift, and calm the soul. The poems themselves are usually "musical" in the commonly understood sense that they are euphonious, metrically regular, and often fit for singing. The main point of these poems, however, is not their own musical form but rather their celebration of music, harmonious sound, that has its origins from natural and artificial sources. Beginning with poems that locate music in the harmony of natural sounds, we discover that White wants very much to retreat from human noise into rural landscapes where he can hear the "wild music" that soothes minds made anxious by the frenzied competition of human endeavor. In this group of poems, nature's music returns its listener to a beauty from which mankind has turned its attention far too long.

The "wild sounds" of the poem beginning "When pride and envy" (p. 80) are sounds heard in the wild, i.e., away from the artificial, mechanical haunts of human activity. The poet desires to return to those scenes of solitude and silence "when pride and envy" imbue his heart "with gall," for only in retreat can he cure himself of the disease that frets modern life, the "getting and spending" that lays "waste our powers," as Wordsworth put it. When he can "hear the forest bee on wing" or "the tinkling waters moan," the poet may feel that "man and noise are far away." Time will be as "sweetly" flowing as the stream itself, and no heavy burden of galling labor to produce according to the round of a clock would slow time to its usual painful creep:

> When pride and envy, and the scorn
> Of wealth, my heart with gall imbued,
> I thought how pleasant were the morn
> Of silence, in the solitude;
> To hear the forest bee on wing;
> Or by the stream, or woodland spring,
> To lie and muse alone—alone,
> While the tinkling waters moan,
> Or such wild sounds arise, as say,
> Man and noise are far away. (ll. 1-10)

In the Tradition of the Beautiful: Poetry for the Ear

This poem is a wishful "thought," occasioned by the reflection that the poet's heart is filling with gall and needs relief. It seems to be unfinished, concluding with a fine image of wind shredding leaves from forest trees or hurling snow "in ten thousand shapes." But in its apparently unfinished state, the poem has a charm that might be lost in any other condition, for it concludes with the speaker trapped by his "thought," his daydream that has taken him far from "man and noise." While he dreams his way into the woods, sweetly passing "the meditative hour," he retreats further in space and time until he thinks himself into a forest cavern. There he can "listen to the shrieking sprites" that ride the wind in its wrecking fury. The poet's wish is, then, not only to retreat from human noise and vicious behavior, but also to destroy in order to create, just as the autumn wind tears away forest leaves and winter storms blast the land with snow, although it may drift "soft and slow" as it creates "ten thousand shapes."

The making of "ten thousand shapes" in "soft and slow" process is something the artist would like to imitate in his own work, which he is better prepared to do by the end of his thoughtful retreat. This poem is not a forced analogy, however, and so it is a more persuasive piece of Romantic meditation than the one called '"To the Herb Rosemary" (p. 166), which self-consciously strives to identify the artistic process with nature's own way to make beauty. This poem belongs to this discussion because it celebrates the discovery of "rosemary" with a "melancholy song" appropriate to the customary use of the flower as a funeral emblem. Such beauty amidst so much waste is the striking feature of the flower discovered in early January, and the poet wants to make for the occasion a song whose "sweet" strain will match the sweet scent of the lovely flower.

The poem moves from a contemplation of the "sweet scented flower" in stanza 1, where the poet makes the rosemary into a "mournful wreath" he wears while singing his "melancholy song," to the second stanza, where he assumes the place of the corpse itself. The sweet fragrance of the rosemary became the sweet strain of the poet's song, and that becomes in stanza 2 the "sweet decaying smell" of "the pale corpse in [its] lonely tomb." Nature, art, and man all yield to the pleasant seduction of death, "so peaceful and so deep." Finally, in the third and last stanza, the poet's song yields its place to nature's music; the moaning wind becomes a "wild requiem" calling the poet to his grave. The sweet fragrance, the sweet strain, and the sweet decay all become one compelling experience of pleasure in beauty that must pass, even as "a dying fragrance [that will be] o'er my ashes shed."

This power of natural sweetness, whether fragrance or sound, could be a function of art as well, something Kirke White aspired to in much of his own poetry but which he had early discovered in the poetry of the Wartons. When he was fourteen, White composed a poem occasioned by his "reading the poems of Warton" (p. 109). In this tribute, White identifies Warton's poetry with a "soothing shell" that White listens to while reclining beside a rural brook. The pleasure of the poet's words merges with the pleasure of the woodland sounds in such a way that White can imagine Warton a pastoral poet of classic simplicity, "attuning sweet the Dorian reed" while he "softly sings" or plays "the pastoral pipe." Suddenly, though, "the soothing scene is o'er," and White feels transported by "a bolder sweep" of Warton's music:

> But, ah! the soothing scene is o'er,
> On middle flight we cease to soar,
> For now the muse assumes a bolder sweep,
> Strikes on the lyric string her sorrows deep,
> In strains unheard before.
> Now, now the rising fire thrills high,
> Now, now to heaven's high realms we fly,
> And every throne explore:
> The soul entranced, on mighty wings,
> With all the poet's heat upsprings,
> And loses earthly woes;
> Till all alarmed at the giddy height,
> The Muse descends on gentler flight,
> And lulls the wearied soul to soft repose. (ll. 23-36)

Thus may sweet harmonies and soothing sounds give way, abruptly, to "strains unheard before." These are the pleasures of "the ode sublime," another of Warton's kind of poetry that White much admired. Such transport is brief, though intense and exhilarating. White compares it to soaring above the "middle flight" of pastoral music, flying high to heaven's realms "on mighty wings." He will himself often attempt such high flights of visionary poetry, but for the most part and for most mortal listeners, the poet must gently descend, returning his listener to the "soft repose" of his earlier condition. The way the poet achieves these startling effects on (fourteen-year-old) Kirke White is comparable with the way a musician gently strokes his lyre, then suddenly sweeps its strings with bold and vigorous rhythms. In this poem at least, White grants the fact that poetry, as music, cannot only soothe the troubled soul (an achievement that nature's music can also boast) but, if more boldly accomplished, can also, as music, lift the soul above nature itself, can raise the mind to heights of vision that leave behind any need for sweetness and soothing sounds.

It is a fact for the boy Kirke White that Warton's sublime odes could entrance him in the manner of powerful music, and it is the constantly tempting possibility for the young man Kirke White that he could also compose a poetry that does the same for its readers. Like Warton before him, White would have to begin with "middle flight" and soft songs with sweet and pleasing themes before he could soar on a "bolder sweep." Beauty was to be a preparation for sublimity, just as music might be the most reliable means for enjoying that beauty. Thus White courts music in all its forms, from natural sounds to sophisticated organ pieces, for its power to soothe and bring the soul into beautiful harmony with the order of all creation.

In his unfinished poem beginning "O give me music" (p. 98) he calls again for some escape from the "noise and care" of life's common chaos, hoping for the same retreat to rural peace that he imagined in his poem "When pride and envy." But in this poem, giving himself to music, to an actual form of art rather than to a wishful thought (as in the poem discussed at the beginning of this section), he is taken beyond the realm he hoped for in the earlier poem. The music he hears changes from an "air of peace, some dying plaint" into a "choral train" that carries his spirit aloft, "beyond the skies, and leaves the stars behind." Music is nearly always a mediate form, a means of transport, for White; the order of music, a harmony of sound, is designed to achieve an effect that defeats all order, both natural and artistic. And so music as beauty seems to be no more an end in itself than does sleeping: both are preparations for efforts of greater ambition.

And night is no time for sleeping in most of White's poetry, for the evening and midnight consitute the ideal conditions for the solitary to assert himself: there is little resistance by others or other forms to his insistence upon the priority of his own identity. Thus, in such a poem as "Solitude" (p. 93) or "'To a Taper" (p. 186), where the chief experience of sensation is sight, the speaker becomes increasingly conscious of the vast nothingness and darkness surrounding him and underlying all existence; his dread is that he may be himself, in essence, no more than the darkness pressing in upon him. To combat such depression, the poet of vision must either keep on the move (as in "Clifton Grove") or emphasize the imagery of movement that passes before his eyes, thus assuring himself that reality is in process, capable of transformation and perhaps release for himself.

At night, however, when darkness prevails, the importance of sight diminishes while the value of sound increases. Then nature's music can best be heard, and it soothes troubled spirits, even reassures them that they are at one with the harmonious process of her reality. In poems such as "To Midnight" (p. 151) and "The Shipwrecked Solitary's Song to the Night" (p. 212), White celebrates the special providence of night and darkness as a time of sweet assurance. He joins his song to nature's in these poems. Not all persons will find midnight and evening reassuring (as indeed in some of his own poems White does not), but to "philosophic souls" they "speak . . . delight." Appearance of the moon in "To Midnight" and the first star in "The Shipwrecked Solitary's Song" evoke hymns of contentment from the poet. In such moods, points of light become signals of triumph over fear; they are especially hailed as summonses to *thought* ("pensive orb") or to *dream* ("pleasant are my dreams"). Therefore, when the moon appears at midnight, the poet raises his "orisons divine" to "sing the gentle honours of her name." Even the terrors of Superstition are made "gentle" by the special time, when Fancy "pours upon [his] ear her thrilling song." He answers with a tune of his own, a "romantic lay" which he plays upon his flageolet, sending forth pensive music of "sweet notes" that are heard by lonely travelers while crossing the dark moors.

"To Midnight" ends with the perplexing tear, as do so many of White's poems, just at the moment when he casts "a much-meaning glance upon the scene." In this poem he is not content to accept the darkness, to give himself to sound alone. But in

"The Shipwrecked Solitary's Song to the Night," he unabashedly celebrates the darkness itself:

> The dayspring brings not joy to me,
> The moon it whispers not of peace;
> But oh! when darkness robes the heavens,
>   My woes are mixed with joy. (ll. 29-32)

He "weave[s] a song" out of the sweetness of evening's "solemn calm," and he "tune[s] [his] little reed / To hymns of harmony" that were difficult to discern during "the gray morn high." But at night his music is "sweet," for then he thinks that "Aerial voices answer" him, and all join in a great chorus of natural communion.

When he addresses the great Maker behind nature's beauty, White makes his poems into "hymns of harmony," as in "Awake, sweet harp of Judah" (p. 217) and "A Hymn for Family Worship" (p. 218). In both these poems the poet relies on the metaphor of music for achieving the identity of purpose between poetry and religion. He adds a nice touch in the former when he calls for a retuning of the harp, made consonant with the Christian dispensation: "Retune thy strings for Jesus' sake." The new music of Christianity is not only a call for spiritual reassurance, but it is a summons for the spirit to come out of hiding, to leave behind the insecurities and guilts of existence that needs "a hiding place" in the darkness. That White literally sang his own compositions we may gather from a note he added to this hymn: "the last stanza of this hymn was added extemporaneously, by the Author, one summer evening, when he was with a few friends on the Trent, and singing it as he was used to do on such occasions" (p. 218).

He might literally as well have played upon the flageolet, lyre, and harp. But whether he actually played these instruments or not, he often uses them as metaphorical images in his poetry, representing his art of poetry as an art of music. In the ode "To My Lyre" (p. 136) he explains in nine homostrophic stanzas that he is happy with the simple music he can make on his lyre, a "music wild" because it is unsophisticated and natural (not trained). This kind of music suits the individual even though it is not heard by others, or certainly not applauded by the crowd, which gives its attention only to "mightier minstrels harping loud" (l. 8). The speaker has not learned his art from any "academic lore"; he has not learned to create "the solemn strain" or "build the polished rhyme." Instead, he depends on his native talent to "charm" with rustic simplicity:

> Thou simple Lyre! thy music wild
>   Has served to charm the weary hour,
> And many a lonely night has 'guiled,
> When even pain has owned, and smiled,
>   Its fascinating power.
>
> Yet, O my Lyre! the busy crowd
>   Will little heed thy simple tones;
> Them mightier minstrels harping loud
> Engross,—and thou and I must shroud
>   Where dark oblivion 'thrones. (ll. 1-10)

"Rustic swains" believe in the power of such simple music. They have an imaginative faith in its power to "hush the wild winds when they roar,/And still the billowy main." The poet himself trusts natural forces so much that he enjoys the "little dirge" made upon the lyre when it is swept by the "gentle zephyr's wing" without assistance from him. To this extent White shares with his Romantic contemporaries a reliance upon the wind harp as a symbolic metaphor, expressing an ideal of art as simple, low keyed, unencumbered with "academic lore." But White does not ignore the importance of learning, sophistication, and a trained ear.

> Yet dear to me the wreath of bay,
>   Perhaps from me debarred;
> And dear to me the classic zone,
> Which, snatched from learning's laboured throne,
>   Adorns the accepted bard.

He suggests in the last three stanzas of the poem "To My Lyre" that he aspires to compete with the "mightier minstrels." He would like to "dwell / Where Cam or Isis winds along," study at the great English universities of Cambridge or Oxford, and "call the ear of taste / To listen to [his] song." He would not, however, abandon his "simple lyre," his "little friend." Instead, he would change his music to a different tone, "to happier lays" that would cause "the cloistered glooms [to] smile." And what makes him believe that his music would be happier is his belief that *he* would be a happy man if he could hear himself praised by cultivated audiences. This poem is a poignant tribute to White's ambition, to his faith in education as well as to his appreciation for the charm of simplicity.

If he could unite thought, or intellect, with simplicity, White would achieve the ideal form to which his art aspires. When he hears the music of others, of those "mightier minstrels" like the Wartons, he hears the simplicity of nature's music made significant by the thoughtfulness of man. Most of reality is a chaos of sound and frantic waste of power, and so it is the obligation of the artist to rescue the power from dissipation and to give the chaos a shape. When he calls for music, as in his fragmentary poem "O give me music" (p. 98), White is crying out for relief from the tawdriness of everyday existence. It is a cry we have often heard in his writing, both prose and poetry. "O give me music—for my soul doth faint; / I'm sick of noise and care." He needs beauty, the reassurance that some more important reality exists, is possible: "some air of peace," or a "choral train" that weaves sound into "mellow" music, "floating paeans" filling the "buoyant wind." These are clearly escapist urges, but the escape would be honorable because it would be an act of defiance rather than retreat. For some, discretion is the greater part of valor, but for the artist that is in Kirke White's soul, submission to the ugly world of commerce and litigation would be not only cowardly but also unrealistic.

He claims that he has left behind the less realistic urges of his artistic impulse, "when high romance o'er every wood and stream / Dark lustre shed" (p. 100). Now that his "pensive lyre" has awakened, he has passed beyond the threshold of "mystery" into a realm of "sobered thought." Such is the burden of this fragmentary poem that anticipates Keats (in, for example, "On Sitting Down to Read *King Lear* Again"). White discovers quickly that leaving behind the forest of romance is dangerous to the imagination, for "sobered thought" may be a greater foe to art than is shoddy reality. A series of unfinished poems (pp. 98-101) suggests that White was experiencing the difficulty of composition while conscious of his advance beyond "high romance." He tells us that his lyre is "hushed" (p. 99), that his hand has been "robbed of its cunning" and so it must retire from the task of making music. Those "pensive wires" have ceased to raise the spirit that once danced to "forest melodies" of rustic simplicity. In the final stanza of this fragment, he suddenly changes his metaphor from the lyre to "withering flowers of poesy." Since the poem is unfinished, we cannot tell for certain what the poet is up to here, but he has abandoned his lyre in favor of "flowers of poesy," however withered they may be. Sweet music has ceased, and in the silence he takes up dying flowers; the fragrance, however, lingers and in that image White takes yet another step away from the substantiality of art, from sight to sound to fragrance. Rather than make too much of this slight detail from an unfinished poem, we can merely notice it as one of many ways White attempts to hold onto something valuable that seems to be slipping away from him as he grows older.

In two otherwise unrelated lyrics, he begins his songs with phrases that echo the opening of Milton's "Lycidas": "Once more, and yet once more" (p. 100), and "Yes, once more that dying strain" (p. 207). Both poems are poignant expressions of loss, though not the profound loss Milton describes in "Lycidas." For White's loss is not of life, but of confidence (hinted at in some letters he wrote while studying at Winteringham in 1805, when he refers to his "poor neglected muse" and his fear that poetry "may desert [him] forever!").[9] This is not to say that the loss of his confidence is not serious, and it is not to say that the threat to his imagination represented by such loss is not comparable with the experiences described in Milton's elegy, for White explicitly invited such comparison. White's two short lyrics (one is unfinished) lack the richness and polish of Milton's poem, but they are not without emotional power.

> Once more, and yet once more,
>   I give unto my harp a dark woven lay;
> I heard the waters roar,
>   I heard the flood of ages pass away.

This may remind us of critical moments when artists such as Coleridge (in his "Dejection" ode) and Wordsworth (in his "Resolution and Independence") are tested by their imaginations to overcome self-doubt and even despair.

The poignance of White's little poem comes from its utter *pastness*, for it tries to recover the richness of roaring waters and flooding spirit with this "dark woven lay." If he cannot do it for himself, he can call upon others: "Yes, once more that dying strain, / Anna, touch thy lute for me," he asks in a poem expressing the very sweetness it claims to hear in Anna's music. It does for the reader what the poet claims for himself from Anna's music; it creates a "Sweet . . . melody," "mildly soft" with a "friendly ray." The simple tones of a pensive lyre are possible, but they are difficult to accomplish. Indeed, White concentrates most of his talents on efforts in different directions—all designed to accommodate his increasingly self-conscious maturity of imagination. While other poems suggest that he may have abandoned simplicity for sophistication, in no other poems is White more moving with the poignance of his loss than in these short, sometimes unfinished, verses to his lyre.

His concern that he may be losing something essential for his art is suggested by a phrase White uses in two of the poems to be examined next: "the frozen ear." This phrase intends to convey the experience of terror, evoked by something heard, and so it does, but it also captures the poet's own fear that he may be on the wrong track with his art, if not in his life. The critical moment comes when he must ask himself if he can no longer hear the sweet music of nature, of simple art, and if he can not himself make that same sweet music from simple forms. Like Wordsworth and Coleridge, White realized that one such form is the ballad; it is capable of the thoughtfulness he desired; and it is for poetry the unsophisticated instrument that the lyre is for music. White does not make "lyrical ballads," but he experiments in the form nevertheless.

"Thought" and "pensiveness" usually suggest "solemnity" and "melancholy" to Kirke White. These are qualities he found difficult to express in lyrical poems, which ought to be "happy" and cheerful, soothing with their rustic melodies. As he developed his art, he increasingly (or, rather, more often) looked in the direction of blank verse as more appropriate for the solemn thought that maturity demanded from his muse. The night was not always a time of serene calm (as in "To Midnight"); sometimes it is stormy, making music more like a dirge than a hymn (as in "To the Wind, at Midnight," p. 163). Nature's music is a "howl," then, a "howling sweep," a "sudden rush" pouring forth a "hollow dirge." To capture this sound White experiments in several ways, realizing that what he is after is a new tone—no longer the sweet pensiveness of his rustic lyre.

The fragment beginning "The western gale, / Mild as the kisses of connubial love" (p. 110) is an interesting exploration of new territory. White composes in blank verse to convey his realization that a different form is required for a harsher sound, a music unlike the sweet harmonies we have been examining so far. In this poem he frames his new thought with an old situation: lolling beside a woodland stream while listening to the soothing sounds of nature. From an atmosphere of mild play, languid feelings, security amidst velvet turf, and lulling sounds of insects, he must escape to a more vigorous life of the imagination (a situation James Thomson developed in *The Castle of Indolence*). The poet must resist the temptation to slumber amidst sensuous comfort, for that might mean his imaginative death. He must address the "frozen ear" with discord and hollow tones if he is to capture the fullness of a reality made melancholy by pensiveness.

Lolling at his solitary ease, the poet suddenly hears the pealing of bells from a distance. They "rise with gradual swell" and then "die upon the pensive ear, / Melting in faintest music." (ll. 17-21). They must die on the ear of thought because they announce a festival that can be enjoyed to the fullest only by people still living with "Superstition":

> Such is the jocund wake of Whitsuntide,
> When happy Superstition, gabbling eld!
> Holds her unhurtful gambols. All the day
> The rustic revellers ply the mazy dance
> On the smooth shaven green, and then at eve
> Commence the harmless rites and auguries;
> And many a tale of ancient days goes round. (ll. 26-32)

In such passages as this White feels heavily the weight of the past for a modern poet who can no longer "believe" literally in the tales of romance and mystery. Although he is unwilling to admit, with some of his contemporaries, that Christianity is quite as much a product of superstition as any other story of miracle and mystery, White comes very close at times to realizing that he must hold to *some* myth if he is to keep his imagination alive at all; like Wordsworth, he would "rather be a Pagan suckled on a creed outworn" than "lay waste" his powers and not be able to see in Nature the much that "is ours." To see this, however,

White retains his Christian faith, much qualified by his faith in reason as well as by his natural piety.

Indeed, he cries out in this poem, "Ignorance! Thou art fallen man's best friend" (ll. 42-43). At this stage of his growth, White fears that all joy and happiness in art or in life are functions of superstition and ignorance, beyond which he must pass. What is left to him, then, as for all mature artists, is a harsher truth, a sharper "happiness" that the refined sense affords. Realizing that he must make his way alone, apart from the social happiness of those rustics who still enjoy the revels of Whitsuntide, he is tempted to "forsake the world" utterly and flee more deeply into the forest. But he is brought back to his responsibility by his reason and his experience; "the distant prospect always seems more fair" (58). He will have to live with his heritage of reason mixed with faith, and he will have to use his talent to please with truth, however harsh its music may sound to the "frozen ear" (l. 42)

When one hears a sound that he does not like, that terrifies him, or that displeases him, he hears with "a frozen ear": this is the import of the phrase in White's ballad narrative of "Gondoline" (p. 192). But "the frozen ear" may also indicate an incapacity to imagine, an inability to hear certain pitches, certain melodies, and it is this possible meaning in the phrase that gives it some richness of ambiguity. In the ballad, however, little ambiguity is attached to the phrase when the poet uses it to describe Gondoline's reaction to the "mysterious sounds" she hears from deep in the cavern she has just entered (p. 194; ll. 61-62). She is startled by the sounds, but she has nevertheless followed her curiosity, begun to explore a darkness inviting her into its mystery, and that speaks well of her capacity to imagine. If anything, her hearing will be improved too well for her sanity; her frozen ear will not handicap her imagination, although it will destroy her reason. Gondoline expresses White's own fear that too much imagination is dangerous, but at the same time she reveals his fascination with the realm of the supernatural, of the great mystery at the heart of reality. He explores the cave with Gondoline, and as she moves deeper into its darkness, he imagines all the horrors she witnesses; White may even enjoy narrating the horrors with more zest than he should, but he has control of his interest through his choice of form and tradition. The ballad was not out of bounds for tales of the supernatural and horrible (it "supplied a structural and dramatic device for effectively employing the unearthly").[10] White could, therefore, without violating his sense of decorum, indulge his interest through it.

The ballad itself is ably composed, with little that is "lyrical" about it in the Wordsworthian sense (although perhaps in the Coleridgean sense). It is made up of seventy-three ballad stanzas (four lines rhyming *abab* in alternating lengths of four and three feet) telling a story that moves economically through six parts. In the first part (ll. 1-40) the setting is described as a moonlit beach where a lovely maiden is roaming alone; she is obviously anxious, wan of face, and looking often out to sea as though expecting someone or something to arrive. She has often roamed this beach, and she has been looking for her beloved Bertrand, who has "gone to the Holy Land / To fight the Saracen" (ll. 15-16). She has placed a light high up on the rocks to guide her lover home, but she is despairing of ever seeing him again.

In the next part (ll. 41-65) she discovers a cave in the cliff's side, ominously described:

> And pendant from its dismal top
> The deadly nightshade hung;
> The hemlock and the aconite
> Across the mouth were flung. (ll. 45-48)

Undeterred, Gondoline enters the cave, as though drawn into it by "some deep-working charm." She sees a snake and steps on a toad, but nothing stops her progress as she moves deeper and deeper into the cavern. Suddenly she hears "mysterious sounds" upon "her frozen ear" (ll. 61-62), sounds of laughter accompanied by thunder. The "charm" leads her on, "though each big glaring ball of sight / Seemed bursting from her head" (ll. 71-72). At this point White adds a note to explain that he gets his image of the "ball of sight [that] seemed bursting from her head" from Collins's *Ode on the Passions*, and with this note he betrays one of his motives for the poem (as well as exhibiting his learning); the subtitle for Collins's poem is "An Ode for Music," and as such it not only celebrates the power of music to raise passion, but it also warns of the destructiveness which unleashed passion can wreak. The "charm" that draws Gondoline to her destruction is equivalent to the "music" that raises the passions in Collins's ode.

But this is not an explicit point of White's ballad, only something he hints at with his note to explain why Gondoline should be so frightened. Suddenly she sees a "pale blue light" which bursts "full a flood of flame." In the third part (ll. 77-108) she discovers a coven of witches met to celebrate their latest gory exploits. Gondoline is possessed by the "charm" that holds her to the spot, as she watches the "twelve withered witches" dancing around a boiling cauldron. Suddenly they stop for each "to tell what she had done," and Gondoline leans forward "to hear the dreadful tale" of each witch in turn. She is, like Coleridge's Wedding Guest, forced against her will to listen to tales of supernatural terror, but she will not survive to hear twelve such tales.

In the fourth part (ll. 109-68) she hears the first tale. This witch tells how she has slowly tortured and then murdered a group of shipwrecked survivors drifting about in a boat. First she, in the guise of the wind, yanked an infant from its mother's arms and drowned it in the ocean; then she "throttled" a young man being held by his father. Finally, she bored a hole in the boat and drowned all the others. Nature was her accomplice, and nature sang for her a funeral song. The first witch ends her story by throwing into the cauldron a bit of the infant's hair which she held onto when she yanked it overboard into the sea. Then the second witch tells how she enticed a girl to murder her mother so that she could "wanton with her lover" (l. 184)., In order to cut her mother's throat, the girl had to cut through three of her mother's fingers which are the contribution made by the second witch to the cauldron:

> And she threw the fingers in the fire,
> The red flame flamed high,
> And round about the cauldron stout
> They danced right merrily. (ll. 213-16)

Then, with little forewarning, the third witch rises to tell her tale. Only because she is the third, one of the more powerful numbers, should we be alert to her tale as anything special. Since the first two tales are among the more horrible to human imagination, the third could not be particularly shocking: but to Gondoline it is. For this is the story of how her lover was killed in battle. The witch tells how she tempted Bertrand to his death by saying that his fiancée had already married during his absence. He, in passion, threw himself into battle, "And soon all mangled o'er with wounds/He on the cold turf bled." The witch "tore/His head" from his body, brought it to this cavern, and here displays it before tossing it into the boiling cauldron. This is exactly what Gondoline feared, as she had earlier leaned forward better to hear the third witch's tale:

> Now Gondoline, with fearful steps,
>   Drew nearer to the flame,
> For much she dreaded now to hear
>   Her hapless lover's name. (ll. 221-24)

Gondoline's reaction upon seeing her lover's head constitutes the last section of the ballad (ll. 261-92). As soon as she saw it, she screamed and fell forward into the witches' ring while thunder and laughter rang about her. The "mysterious sounds" were heard all around her as she fell in a faint, then when she awoke "all was stillness there." We are back, then, to the beginning scene, when the moon shines "sweetly" into the cave, revealing a river that runs through it. The girl, believing that her lover is dead, leaps to her death and is "seen no more.—But oft/Her ghost is known to glide/At midnight's silent, solemn hour,/Along the ocean's side" (ll. 290-92). The ballad ends, then, with a supernatural confirmation of the importance of the spot where passion was charmed to its destruction.

The interesting points in this ballad are, apart from the narrative skill, (1) the ambiguity of the meaning that derives from the point of view, and (2) the symbolic imagery of the cave, the charm, and the frozen ear. We are never sure if this is only a dream by Gondoline or if it is a real experience, for when she awoke she immediately killed herself, "fired" by "madness" (l. 283). It was her way of ending the anxiety she felt while awaiting her lover's long-delayed return; it was the only resolution to desperately unrequited love; it was a nightmare realization of impatient fear. We simply do not know why Gondoline killed herself, for certain; to believe that she saw witches, heard gory tales, and discovered her lover's bloody death is to accept the story as a reasonable account of death, brought about by forces of evil bent upon torment and pain. But we know that Gondoline is distraught, and as a creature enslaved by her passion she is not to be trusted entirely as a credible witness.

On the other hand, we have no reason to distrust the poet. For him, this woman is entirely credible. She is driven by her fear into a darkness that all too many human beings know, a darkness of fearful mystery, haunted by irrational forces of destruction. When she descends into the cave, she is (for us) clearly exploring her own state of mind, her own passion of anxiety. Her courage is a product of the "charm" that protects her from her reason, from the guard against destructiveness. She is not long stalled by the terror that strikes her "frozen ear." Indeed, she pursues the sound until she arrives at its source, a source of disgusting evil and disrespect for life, as infancy, old age, or love. Here is a fearful region to explore, but its reality is something White refuses to ignore.

If this is beauty, it is not the beauty of soothing, calming sweetness that he knew to celebrate in such poems as he composed to his lyre. In the only other poem that White calls a "ballad," he pleads with the "bitter winds" to "be hushed, be hushed" (p. 203). In this he imagines the plight of an abandoned mother, wishing only for death as a release from the misery her lover's absence has left her in. The music of nature is a mockery of her unhappiness, tempting her to murder and suicide:

> Oh, that I were but in my grave,
>   And winds were piping o'er me loud,
> And thou, my poor, my orphan babe,
>   Wert nestling in thy mother's shroud!

The security of death is all that remains for the abandoned woman. Death is always an ambivalent fact for White, and this poem exploits that ambivalence. In it, death is a release from pain, but it is also a harsh alternative to the love that might have been. It is not to be preferred, but it is not to be denied, either. Nature's music has become a dance of death.

This is Kirke White's constant refrain, the theme of his melancholy existence. It inevitably leads him to the brink of despair, where he tries boldly to make a poetry of reality, as in his strange "Commencement of a Poem on Despair" (p. 112). In this poem, fifty-seven lines of blank verse, White declares that he will leave behind the "Aonian lyres of silver sound," with their "softest harmony" and "sounds of pleasure." Instead, he must "strike the strings of dissonance" to imitate the new found reality of nature's "hollow tones." He must, like nature, "howl forth his sufferings to the moaning wind," give voice to "discord in the sound." The vision of Gondoline is also the vision of Kirke White, for he has discovered at the heart of reality a fearful witches' sabbath. Thus he must sing of Despair, imitate the "infernal chorus," and join "the dreadful song" with "shouts, screams, and agonizing shrieks." He is on the verge of discovering the importance of an authentic voice, even if it sounds (to convention) like madness. As in the poem on "The Eve of Death" (p. 114), White confronts the "void" that "foreruns a storm" (l. 3). Even this void, this "silence," is potentially a new song, when "the harp's unvisited strings / Sound sweet, as if swept by a whispering breeze." Something not yet done is always capable of being better done, as Keats would later celebrate in his "Ode on a Grecian Urn."

II Odes and Elegies: Simple Tones and Lofty Strains

To achieve "lofty strains" with "simple tones" is an admirable goal, one which Kirke White only occasionally succeeded in reaching. The most common form to use for achieving lofty strains in eighteenth-century English poetry was the ode, for as Norman Maclean observed in his classic study of the subject, "the Great Ode had been identified with the sublime almost as soon as England was aware of both; toward the end of the eighteenth century, after the beautiful came to be commonly viewed as an aesthetic completion of the sublime, the lesser lyric was identified with the lesser aesthetic pleasure."[11] The "lesser" ode tended, in form, to be Horatian, with homostrophic verses, while the "Great" ode was likely to be Pindaric, with its exacting, intricate scheme of interlocking triads (something that White did not attempt).

The ode was a very popular form throughout the century, from Dryden's magnificent ones "for St. Cecilia's Day" and "Alexander's Feast," to Wordsworth's "Intimations of Immortality" and "To Duty"; later than White, of course, were to be created some of the greatest in the language, by John Keats, but earlier, in mid-century, were some interesting and pleasing experiments in odes on "several descriptive and allegoric subjects" (as Collins called them) by William Collins and Joseph Warton. It was to these odes by Collins and Warton especially, with backward glances at Milton, that Kirke White looked for models for

In the Tradition of the Beautiful: Poetry for the Ear

imitation. That is not surprising, for, as Maclean says, "the later eighteenth century agreed that with Collins and Gray (and such lesser figures as Joseph Warton and Akenside) a new school of ode writers had arrived, their creations marking a renaissance in" the use of that form.[12]

Whether it was Collins's "Ode to Evening" and Warton's "Ode to Solitude," or Collins's "Ode to Pity" and Warton's "Ode to Fancy," White had before him fine examples of polished, urbane verse to imitate. These poems are not much read or admired today, but for readers of poetry in White's time they were not only pleasing to read, they were inspiring as disciplined ways to express emotions and feelings not appropriate to heroic couplets or blank verse. The ode is very close in form and intent to the "song," deriving as it does from the Greek word for singing. It is not surprising then to find so many poets, like White, using metaphors of music to build their odes, sometimes even expecting their poems to be set to music for performance (as were Dryden's and Collins's). While none of Kirke White's odes has been set to music, they might very well have been sung, literally as well as figuratively, by the young poet himself.

White composed at least nineteen odes, most of which use music as a major source of imagery for their construction. This music ranges from the simple tones of "To My Lyre" (p. 136) to the lofty strains of "'Genius" (p. 154), but the dominant tone is a subdued, quiet tone of simplicity, a tone quite appropriate to the dominant form, the Horatian. (We should remember that one of his earliest poems was a translation of "an ode of Horace into English verse . . . for the Monthly Preceptor.")[13] In his tour de force "To Contemplation" (p. 145), White covers the entire range of music in this, the longest of his odes (154 lines): seeking the constant companionship of Contemplation, he calls upon that "pensive sage" to accompany him on a daylong walk through the countryside and then into the city at night.,

They will begin their walk to the tunes of the lark's "matin song" (l. 22), harmonized with "the herdsman's oaten quill" (l. 26), and then they will listen to "the little peasant's song" at noon (l. 39); as evening draws on, they may hear "the weary rustic" "whistle his wild melody" (ll. 53-54), and then "the distant sounds of pastoral lute" (l. 79) will "rise upon our wandering ear." Finally, as the evening yields to darkness they may go off to "the busy town" after all are asleep, and there they can go into the church to enjoy its awesome echoes as they pace its "long reluctant aisle" (l. 136).

This poem, in octosyllabic couplets, derives from the popular tradition of imitating Milton's companion pieces "L'Allegro" and "Il Penseroso." White echoes Milton's settings and some of his themes, but he tries to "improve" Milton by combining the two poems into one, with a decided preference for "Il Penseroso" as a better companion for Contemplation. White, like Collins in the "Ode to Evening" and Joseph Warton in his "Ode to Fancy," records significant sounds as signals of the harmony in which he participates. Like Collins and Warton, White personifies the power which he invokes, but he does not make it resident in the landscape as does Collins. While he summons Contemplation to accompany him, as Warton does when he calls upon Fancy, White differs importantly from Warton in two respects: he makes Contemplation an equal, as a companion, not a guide, and he does not lose control to enthusiasm, giving way to expressions of wild sentiment and cheap diction. Warton tells how, midway through his poem, he feels when he enters "charnels and the house of woe":

> Now let us louder strike the lyre,
> For my heart glows with martial fire;
> I feel, I feel, with sudden heat,
> My big tumultuous bosom beat;
> The trumpet's clangours pierce my ear;
> A thousand widows' shrieks I hear. (ll. 77-82)

From this point on the poem must be anticlimactic, as it is. White is capable of similar pyrotechnics, but his control is usually great enough to avoid the silliness such tricks can lead to.

"Contemplation" is White's term for controlled fancy, that is, imagination conditioned by thought (or melancholy). His poem is an exercise in restraint, celebrating (as it notices) the music of nature and humanity surrounding him while accompanied by Contemplation. However, we must note the important point that frames the poem: distance from the crowds, "far from noise and riot rude." The poet calls Contemplation from its usual solitude only long enough to join him for this day's walk, but to keep Contemplation beside him, he must himself keep at some distance from the very persons whose music he will celebrate.

In the Tradition of the Beautiful: Poetry for the Ear

Not only is the herdsman whose oaten quill they enjoy on "the plain below," but the lark whose matin song they hear is up among "the floating clouds." Keeping his remove from direct contact is essential for the poet to enjoy the sounds, the "music of humanity," as Wordsworth called it; otherwise, it would be a "noise and riot rude." When he enters the church, unlike Warton's speaker when he does the same, White paces the aisle "with reverence meet," but to be able to do so he must be there alone, with only his thought for companionship:

> Let us in the busy town,
> When sleep's dull streams the people drown,
> Far from drowsy pillows flee,
> And turn the church's massy key;
> Then, as through the painted glass
> The moon's faint beams obscurely pass,
> And darkly on the trophied wall
> Her faint, ambiguous shadows fall,
> Let us, while the faint winds wail
> Through the long reluctant aisle,
> As we pace with reverence meet,
> Count the echoings of our feet,
> While from the tombs, with confessed breath,
> Distinct responds the voice of death. (ll. 127-40)

The poem's structure is the simple one of a walking tour through the countryside and back to the city at night, ending in a moonlit church. But as in Milton's two great poems, this one makes its appeal as a meditation that reveals the speaker's developing state of mind, reflected by the sights and then, especially, sounds he experiences during his walk. He is able to carry the morning's light with him into the very evening, into the darkness itself, where shades of death haunt his fancy, because his contemplative habit strengthens his religious faith, symbolized by the church where he ends his tour. His poetry, like the music he hears all around him, is an ordering of his life that prepares him for the darkness with its threat of disintegration and chaos:

> If thou, mild sage, wilt condescend
> Thus on my footsteps to attend,
> To thee my lonely lamp shall burn

> By fallen Genius' sainted urn,
> As o'er the scroll of Time I pore,
> And sagely spell of ancient lore,
> Till I can rightly guess of all
> That Plato could to memory call,
> And scan the formless views of things;
> Or, with old Egypt's fettered kings,
> Arrange the mystic trains that shine
> In night's high philosophic mine;
> And to thy name shall e'er belong
> The honours of undying song. (ll. 141-54)

White does not use the ode for sublimity, nor usually for the enthusiasm that often accompanies or signals the sublime. This avoidance is not typical of most odes in the eighteenth century, especially if they were of the regular Pindaric, or "Great," kind that celebrated the divine; it was left to the "lesser" Horatian kind to be beautiful.[14] However, even in the less subdued form of the irregular Pindaric, White avoids the sublime. He comes closest in an ode to "Genius" (p. 154), which will be examined later, but for the most part his odes are songs of soothing harmony, celebrations of natural beauty, or low-toned, controlled complaints against the world's harsh treatment of genius and talent. His odes are, as a group, poems of beauty rather than poems of sublimity.

"To the Harvest Moon" (p. 163) illustrates his tone of simplicity and style of restrained dignity. It celebrates the festival of harvest-home as a time of "the tripping dance, the exhilarating song" (l. 8), and "the nightingale's enchanting tune" (l. 58). While it is composed as an address to the moon, the poem moves from the joyful singing and dancing of people celebrating the harvest to concentrate on the speaker's own private pleasure in hearing the "enchanting tune" of the nightingale. It does not avoid completely the company of other persons (as does "To Contemplation"), for its very occasion is the happiness of the human community at harvest time, but the poem comes to rest, to its quiet close, with a by-now characteristic feature of White's poetry: the retirement from crowds, called here "sons of luxury" (l. 48), into the speaker's own festival beneath the harvest moon. *His* festival is no tripping dance or exhilarating song, and his dreams are not "of crowded barns"; the poet's equivalent of harvest time is to muse "high on holy themes,/While on the gale / Shall softly sail / The nightingale's enchanting tune" (ll. 55-58).

The fruit of his labor is his art, inspired by the lovely music of nature conditioned by "Contemplation's dreams" (l. 54). The poet's harvest moon is, then, a light of fancy breeding beauty. "To the Harvest Moon" is one of White's happiest poems, but, in his rare use of the epigraph for this poem, he hints at a warning that lies behind the contentment of the poem: citing lines from Virgil (Book I of the *Georgics*, ll. 313-15 and 343), White establishes the pagan background for the harvest-home festival, but because the passage he cites is Virgil's warning that the corn-goddess must be honored if the crops are to be protected from destruction, White suggests that no fruit is safe unless it is protected by ritual and ceremony—thus perhaps a subtle point that art, as ritual, is such a protection. The only clear hint in the poem that destruction is warded off by ceremony comes when the husbandman lies asleep, dreaming of his "crowded barns," and the poet asks that "no hurricane destroy / His visionary views of joy" (ll. 44—45); surely the parallel instance in the next stanza, where the poet is "wrapped in Contemplation's dreams" (l. 54), invites a similar plea for protection from destruction.

The chaos that underlies all life and beauty is a constant and lurking theme in White's poetry, often the result of his own experience of illness and pain but also the result of his religious and philosophical habit of mind. In a poem connected by subject matter with "To the Harvest Moon," entitled "On Whit-Monday" (p. 161), the poet hears the "merry bells" as their happy music falls on his "musing ear." He knows the sound, a celebration of "an ancient holiday" when "rural revels are begun" "on the smooth shaven green." For him, however, the music of the bells has a mournful tone, reminding him of the deaths of all those who formerly celebrated this same holiday. The poet does not wish to spoil the occasion for others (for the happy rustics, that is); he knows the value of seizing the day for whatever pleasure it can provide:

> Mortals! be gladsome while ye have the power,
> And laugh and seize the glittering lapse of joy;
>   In time the bell will toll
>   That warns ye to your graves. (ll. 25-28)

To protect the happiness of the occasion, he will leave the scene even as he looks behind "to where the steeple loud" is still ringing out its jubilee, though for him it is a forlorn sound.

This ode is a keenly self-conscious one in which the poet realizes that his own state of mind, filled as it is with thoughts of mortality, conditions all that he experiences. In it White is able to set off in a kind of tension the opposing values of community happiness and individual sorrow, but little of the tension survives as he makes of himself, a man of feeling, a culture hero: one who, like Aeneas, bears with him wherever he goes a knowledge of the tears that are in all things ("lacrimae rerum"). And so he, the poet, suffers while others enjoy their being. We may feel somewhat embarrassed by this posture (one much criticized in Shelley), but it was conventional for the Age of Sensibility in which White grew up. We may, nevertheless, respect him for his way of presenting the posture in this poem, where he has his speaker take himself away from the revelry so as not to spoil the holiday. That is the kind of discipline and decorum that marks White as an artist rather than an exhibitionist.

He has less reserve in speaking of his private sufferings in his ode "To the Morning: Written during Illness" (p. 167). Even here, however, he subordinates his personal feelings of pain to the larger pattern of harmony and happiness represented by the lovely daybreak. The poem is an exercise in the pathetic, for it appeals to sympathy for the suffering speaker. What saves it from bathos is a kind of undercurrent of vigor felt by the speaker as he looks out upon the scene of life spreading before him. In the other poems we have been examining, White set up scenes of community health and happiness as a counterpoint to his private sense of sorrow; in this one, he reverses the procedure somewhat, as he makes his own illness the occasion for the poem, but weaves through his lines a motif of health and vigor that better define his own predicament.

Nature promises something better than the poet possesses at the moment: "The fresh gale o'er the green lawn breathes; / It fans my feverish brow,—it calms the mental strife" (ll. 10-11). Nature summons him from his sickbed with the call of the lark: "The lark has her gay song begun, / She leaves her grassy nest, / And soars till the unrisen sun / Gleams on her speckled breast" (ll. 13-16). He rises to follow, and when he does he experiences "Blithe Health!" He hears the thatcher begin "his whistle on the eaves" and he hears sounds of human industry: "the driver's voice, his carol blithe, / The mower's stroke, his whetting scythe / Mix with the morning's sounds" (ll. 50-52). Such music restores his health, ever to be retained in imagination and in art, so that he will not fall victim to "the silken couch of Sloth," a sickness from which it is difficult to recover (l. 57).

One sickness nature cannot cure, the one sickness to which White uneasily, though readily, admits and from which he cannot recover: his longing for fame and recognition. This is, as Milton puts it in "Lycidas," "that last infirmity of noble mind," although for White it may also be "that first infirmity." He can forgive the ignorant masses for their failure to recognize his talent. He can even celebrate their rustic festivals and superstitious jubilees, but he cannot forgive the world of cultivation, education, and power for its harsh treatment of genius and talent, his own included. He makes this the theme of the next four odes. All four are artifices, or verbal strategies, for facing the world as it is rather than merely berating it for what it is not. They sometimes come perilously close to mere beratement, but White's basic good taste and good sense keep him from going over the edge into ranting and bitterness.

Desire for fame and disappointment at failure to achieve it are a kind of disease for which the only cure may be the disappointment itself, a condition for the humility that comes from resignation. White invokes the therapy of music and makes it a tribute to the order of beauty to which he subordinates his personal ambition. In his "Fragment of an Ode to the Moon" (p. 157), he calls upon the moon to "soothe these discordant tones to rest" (l. 20). The notes of discord are his "pants for fame," but also his disappointment that his childhood happiness no longer attends him (ll. 25-29). Caught between a lost childhood and a yet unrealized reputation, he is a tormented soul, not unlike those Matthew Arnold would later describe as "wandering between two worlds, one dead / The other powerless to be born." The wistfulness of his poem has an edge keener for us than White could have realized when he composed it, for it represents not only his fear but also the fact that he did die unhappy, lost between childhood and an unrealized adulthood.

"Genius" (p. 154) is the ode which comes closest to falling over the edge of taste into the bathos of self-sorrow. It is made up of six stanzas, divided into two sections with three stanzas each.

The strophe of section 1 describes all those "unblessed" souls who go through life without noticing "jarring Discord's inharmonious strife" (l. 3); these are the ones who "smoothly . . . pursue their way / With even tenor and equal breath," ignorant of pain and evil. The antistrophe describes those "whom griefs devour" (l. 11); these are the favored few blessed by Genius. The epode is an address to this "Genius" itself, pleading with it to "hear the plaint by thy sad favourite made" (l. 24).

The strophe of section 2, like its counterpart in section 1, is concerned with those unblessed by Genius; it tells them that they are fortunate not to suffer the pains of genius, with its "feverish study" and "moody fits" (l. 43). The second strophe concentrates, again like its complement in section 1, on the person of Genius, as one dejected and filled with despair. Finally, in the concluding epode, almost twice the length of the epode in section 1, the poem is brought to its resolution with a "proclamation": it is a bill of indictments against all those forces which make Genius unhappy and despairing.

We can read this poem in any of several ways. As irony bordering on sarcasm, it is contemptuous of stupidity and luxury, but so then would it be a lament for a world whose values are so twisted as they seem to be. The irony would have to stop short at the beginning of the second epode:

> By Sulmo's bard of mournful fame,
> By gentle Otway's magic name,
> By him, the youth, who smiled at death,
> And rashly dared to stop his vital breath,
>   Will I thy pangs proclaim. (II, ll. 55-59)

These poets, Ovid, Otway, and Chatterton, all suffered too much for their genius to have gone in vain, and about this White cannot be ironic. The poem could be read as an outpouring of self-pity in which White identifies himself with these three poets, but he never says he wishes he would not have to suffer because of his genius; instead, he wants all to understand that the blessings of genius are at best mixed blessings:

> For still to misery closely thou'rt allied,
> Though gaudy pageants glitter by thy side,
>   And far resounding Fame. (ll. 60-62)

This comes closer to the main tone of the poem. It is both ironic and self-pitying, but its formal balance and drama of point of view keep it within the bounds of good taste. Those of "Genius' favourites" who cannot ignore "jarring Discord's inharmonious strife" may hope for "far resounding Fame," while those without genius or any who only "smoothly . . . pursue their way" will "sink" into glorious darkness. The poet's curse is that he, like Achilles, exchanges a short life for enduring fame. This is the worthy theme of this unrelaxed poem. It serves to remind us that all the time White celebrates the soothing powers of nature's music, its harmonious sounds heard when one is far from human "noise and riot," he must keep in uneasy balance his regard for "jarring Discord's inharmonious strife." White seems always closer and closer to realizing that he must find a new style, a different voice, for mixing the melancholy tones of life's discords with his easy talent for simple elegance of soothing melody. His music must break from its heritage of classical balance, incorporate the discords and risk more for the sake of an enlarging vision of reality.

The best poem in this group of odes on the subject of genius and fame is "To the Earl of Carlisle, K.G." (p. 142). Like the ode to "Genius," this one is also made up of two sections, each with three stanzas. The first section describes the musings of "an humble Poet" dwelling "remote from human noise." He observed the happiness of nature surrounding him and he studied the ways of humanity in ancient history. In the antistrophe of the first section, he cries out with surprise that once Genius was not ignored or poorly regarded by the World as it is in these times; the epode then focuses on examples of those in whom merit and reward were united, Sidney, Sheffield, and Lyttleton, all of whose songs were well tuned and harmonious:

> Yet was the Muse not always seen
> In Poverty's dejected mien,
>   Not always did repining rue,
>   And misery her steps pursue.
> Time was, when nobles thought their titles graced
>   By the sweet honours of poetic bays,
>   When Sidney sung his melting song,
>   When Sheffield joined the harmonious throng,
>   And Lyttelton attuned to love his lays.

> Those days are gone—alas, for ever gone!
> No more our nobles love to grace
> Their brows with anadems, by genius won,
> But arrogantly deem the Muse as base;
> How different thought their sires of this degenerate race! (ll. 21-34)

The second section returns to the present time, where we hear that the modern minstrel sings in "broken measures" his "solitary song" because the world will not make him at home with it. The second antistrophe says, however, that there may be some hope in the example of Carlisle, who has brought back "The Augustan age anew" (l. 48). White refers here to the Augustan age of Rome, not Britain, unless by the term he means to include Elizabeth's reign rather than the period of the Stuart Restoration. Carlisle, then, like Maecenas under the Emperor Augustus, recognizes the merit of genius and so he may be the harbinger of a new age, a renewal of the golden age for the arts:

> But human vows, how frail they be!
> Fame brought Carlisle unto his view,
> And all amazed, he thought to see
> The Augustan age anew.
> Filled with wild rapture, up he rose,
> No more he ponders on the woes
> Which erst he felt that forward goes,
> Regrets he'd sunk in impotence,
> And hails the ideal day of virtuous eminence. (ll. 45-53)

The concluding epode is a turn yet again (and there are several "turns" in this ode, signaled by the words "But," "Yet," "But," and "Yet") to focus on the reality of the present time. Anyone who thinks that a new era of respect for genius is about to begin just because one man of wealth and power is generous, that person is a fool: "Ah! silly man, yet smarting sore / With ills which in the world he bore, / Again on futile hope to rest" (ll. 54—56). What Carlisle represents is more like a flashing comet that heightens the gloom of the darkness through which he passes, not the rising sun of a new day. White brings balance to his poem by repeating the image of the swallow, first noticed by the musing poet at the opening of the poem and lost sight of until the conclusion, when the poet-speaker admonishes the silly man for not knowing that "one swallow makes no summer" (l. 58).

One reason this is a better ode than the others of this group is that it achieves an objectivity lacking in the others, and it achieves its objectivity through a dramatic frame that distinguishes the musing poet from the poet-speaker who sees a larger reality with more experience than the "silly" poet who dreams that Carlisle heralds a new age of Augustus.

Beside the point of the poem's success through greater objectivity than usual, we should not ignore the probability that Kirke White was quite as much the "silly" poet in his poem as he was the maker of the ode about the silly poet. This is one of his strengths, that he is sometimes capable of seeing himself as though from some distance from himself. This capacity is missing from the final ode in this group, "On Disappointment." This poem is about as pure a lyric as we find among White's odes, with little of the possibility for ambiguity of tone or complexity of structure that we can find in the others. It does, however, return us to the main theme of the group: disappointment as a fact of the artist's life and, beyond that, as a fact of life itself. Characteristically, White employs music metaphors to convey this truism, announced by "the lingering knell" of bells that say "hopes are dead" (ll. 12-13). All falls away, even that most precious commodity of the artist: beauty's self must die.

> Oh, what is Beauty's power?
>   It flourishes and dies;
> Will the cold earth its silence break,
> To tell how soft, how smooth a cheek
>   Beneath its surface lies?
>   Mute, mute is all
>   O'er Beauty's fall;
> Her praise resounds no more when mantled in her pall. (ll. 33-40)

The dignity and restraint of this stanza work to control the pain of recognition it contains, a pain reinforced with the point that "music past is obsolete" (l. 43). It is in such passages as this that White approaches the threshold of growth, something he deals with as a matter of changing modes, from the beautiful to the sublime, just as he does when changing from the less uniform picturesque to the more harmonious beautiful. In the next chapter we may see how he manages the sublime, but one point we may anticipate here: that the sublime will not be musical, as harmony, any more than it will be beautiful, as comfort.

Poems that bring comfort to those who grieve others' deaths should be musical, should reassure and sort all things out to make sense of pain and death. Whether music and poetry merely deceive when they do this or whether they impress with a value more compelling than the grief itself, these are questions which the modern poet must entertain. Kirke White, as a professed Christian studying to become a minister, wanted to believe that his poetry could heal the wounds of grief by its message of Christian consolation, but it is a rare thing to find in his collected poetry. Indeed, when he tried to compose an elegy on the death of Nelson, he gave it up as an unfinished fragment; his "Elegy Occasioned by the Death of Mr. Gill" is a wooden, mechanical imitation of the classical form, in the verse style of Gray's famous "Elegy"; and his only completed, forceful elegy, an ode "On the Death of Dermody the Poet," has no consolation.

Again echoing the beginning of "Lycidas," White opens his elegy for Nelson, "Nelsoni Mors" (p. 87), with the staged gesture of "Yet once again, my Harp, yet once again / One ditty more." This does not ring true to feeling, and we are not surprised that the poem is not finished. But White tries heroically to render something fit for the hero's death, relying heavily and frequently upon the symbolic image of the harp to convey the somber tone he wishes to create. When he insists that "he must not sink; . . . he must not, shall not sink" (ll. 15, 16), the young poet embodies his own difficulties in the need to be overly repetitious (however much he may be imitating a great poem). He calls upon Pity to inspire his harp "and give it feeling, which were else too cold / For argument so great" (ll. 40, 41-42). After much reaching (for some insincere words such as "ditty," "freaks," and "kerchiefed") and much imploring for divine assistance, he gives up the attempt. White was too good a poet not to know when he was on a wrong track. Like the Romantic poet he should have become, White spends most of this elegy describing his own state of mind, his own spiritual condition, and to this extent it is worthy of being published with his completed works.

The same kind of faults are present in the one formal elegy White composed for a friend, "Elegy Occasioned by the Death of Mr. Gill, Who Was Drowned in the River Trent, While Bathing, 9th August, 1802" (p. 89). The situation is not promising, and White cannot make much out of it, although he tries for the sake of his friend, to whom he admits in a letter that he was unable "to do justice to your unfortunate friend Gill" (footnote on p. 89). White uses the stanza form of Gray's "Elegy," and again he laces the poem with allusions to Milton's "Lycidas," but again there is little that rings true. He does not offer us Gray's complex pathos or Milton's Christian consolation. What he does offer is to "warble sweet" of Gill on his "sylvan reed." It is difficult to "warble sweet" of someone's death by drowning while bathing.

These last two poems are failures—if not embarrassments—for Kirke White's reputation (lean as it is). But the last poem of this section, the ode "On the Death of Dermody the Poet" (p. 173), is no embarrassment because it is successful as an expression of White's authentic feeling. The feeling is, however, not grief but anger. He describes the lonely death of that young poet with a conviction that makes us think White saw himself in the subject of his poem. The poem has echoes of Collins's "Ode to Fear" in its opening exclamation: "Behold he shrieking passes by: I see, I see him near" (ll. 4-5). The music of this poem is no harmony of sweet sounds; rather, it is a "hollow scream" and "deepening groan" that we hear coming from White as much as from the dying Dermody whose words White captures as they ring upon his ear (ll. 6—7). He images a mock funeral ceremony, where there is no parade of mourners, a fact White ironically deplores as he lists those who should have been present:

> Say, didst thou mark the brilliant poet's death;
>   Saw'st thou an anxious father by his bed,
>   Or pitying friends around him stand:
>   Or didst thou see a mother's hand
>   Support his languid head:
>   Oh none of these—no friend o'er him
>   The balm of pity shed. (ll. 22-28)

The only mourner is the poet's self as he speaks these words, and while he can hear Dermody's "dying scream: Oh God! I hear it still," he will not allow that terror to escape his control. Instead, when he departs, he will "drop one silent tear,/Where lies unwept the poet's fallen head" (ll. 43-44). The gesture is conventional for the age, but the restraint is not always so. Because the rest of the poem is an exercise in disciplined grief, even anger (as later Shelley's will be for the death of Keats), when White exclaims, "Oh God! I hear it still," we believe him. The only music appropriate here is the deep silence that mothers all music.

III   *"Music"*: *The Genius of Sound*

Neither music nor the picturesque has, finally, the power to achieve the ultimate aesthetic pleasure, the sublime, for it requires a dimension of mind, or spirit, that they lack. Purely as a mode of art, without, that is, the associative powers of the mind as audience, the picturesque is a matter of passive sensation, dominated by the faculty of sight. For its part, music is a mode, although more dynamic and plastic than the picturesque, which functions more freely and so most successfully when it lacks "content," the matter of association and connotation; in other words, it is most itself when it is pure form, non-imitative sound, "an unconsummated symbol," as Susanne Langer refers to it.[15] Without association and connotation, poetry could have little or no success in becoming, or communicating, the picturesque, but it could aspire, at least, to becoming music by virtue of its sound patterns alone. As such it is not music, of course, but can nevertheless become a close cousin to music as form, as shaped sound.

Music for Kirke White was a natural kinsman to his own chosen art; he once said that "poetry, painting, and music, are amongst my most delicious and chastest pleasures."[16] He often employs music as a resource of his verse, for imagery and themes, as we have seen. More importantly, it represented for him a symbolic mode or allegorical power to bring the human community into a state of harmony, or to bring the individual soul to a vision of its purpose for being, within the human community or outside it. This function of music, and the poetry that approximates it, produces what we have been calling *beauty*, the experience of proportion, of pieces fitting into their place in a pattern; "the aesthetic of the beautiful was and is a humanizing influence," as Thomas Weiskel puts it.[17] Before such beauty there is merely noise, just as before the picturesque there is only chaos. If music seeks to realize itself as an imitation of the sounds that already exist in nature (as, we might say, a picturesque order), then music becomes little more than picturesque sound; if, on the other hand, it attempts to move beyond the beautiful, the forms of sound, then it passes into a profound silence, just as the picturesque would pass into a profound emptiness, the closest either can come to the sublime.

These speculations were never articulated by Kirke White, but his instincts were true to such directions of thought. He was heir to a tradition of poetry that appropriated the picturesque, as we have seen in the last chapter; he was also heir to an even longer, and perhaps nobler, tradition of poetry that appropriated the beauty of music. This tradition was ancient even by White's time, but of more immediate relevance was its representation in the English poets and musicians from Milton and Purcell to Collins and Handel. In this line of poetry as music are the notable achievements of Milton's "At a Solemn Music" (1633), Dryden's "Song for St. Cecilia's Day" (1687) and "Alexander's Feast" (1697), Handel's music for Dryden's "Alexander's Feast" (1736), and Collins's "The Passions: An Ode for Music" (1747), set to music by William Hayes in 1750. White's own juvenile poem, "Music," should be read, as it undoubtedly was composed, against the background of this beautiful tradition.

To read "Music" (p. 119) this way may expose its derivative character, but we do not expect White's poetry to be very "original" in any significant sense. He was always searching for an authentic voice, but he had the good sense to realize that his search involved much imitation, much practice in the successful techniques of his literary ancestors, before he could begin to challenge them with variations and additions of his own. The phrases, sound patterns, and rhythms, as well as some of the themes, that came to him from the treasury of this English verse and music included Milton's "Sphear-born harmonious Sisters, Voice, and Vers," "divine sounds," "that melodious noise," and "keep in tune with Heav'n" ("At a Solemn Music," ll. 2, 3, 18, and 26); Dryden's "What passion cannot Music raise and quell!," "The Trumpet's loud clangour / Excites us to arms" ("A Song for St. Cecilia's Day," ll. 16 and 25-26); especially important is Dryden's "Alexander's Feast": "sweet the pleasure," "sooth'd with the sound," "soft pity to infuse," "soon he sooth'd his soul to pleasures" (ll. 59, 66, 75, 98), and also this passage:

> Timotheus, to his breathing flute,
>   And sounding lyre,
> Could swell the soul to rage, or kindle soft desire. (ll. 158-60)

The theme of divine inspiration, the idea of poetry's kinship with music ("Voice, and Vers"), the theory of music's action on human passions, the imagery of musical instruments and sounds, and such diction as "sweet," "sooth'd," and "soft": all are elements essential to a poem on music in this tradition, and we find them in White's poem. "Music" is made up of nine quatrains rhyming *abab;* these in turn are arranged in three logically distinguished sections, with four stanzas in each of the first two sections and one in the third. The first section, imitating Dryden's odes, describes the power of music to excite different human passions: "At her command the various passions lie" (l. 5), including care, anger, ecstasy, enthusiasm, ardor, and pity; music moves men to battle *or* to peace, for its essence is indifferent to ethical consequences. But the poet prefers her power for peace:

> Far better she, when, with her soothing lyre,
>   She charms the falchion from the savage grasp,
> And melting into pity vengeful Ire,
>   Looses the bloody breastplate's iron clasp. (ll. 13-16)

The next section betrays White's difference from his classical heritage, for in it he speaks of his own desire for music's companionship, as a means to confirm his spiritual identity. In this he is closer to Collins, with his call for music's return to the modern age ("The Passions," ll. 95-118), but White is less anxious than Collins that music can be heard again in all its significant forms. He is, perhaps even more so than Collins, a victim of an era that Bertrand Bronson described as "discontented, restless, uncommitted, unwilling to stay, yet undetermined to go," even while "it is generally well-mannered and decorous—over-decorous, some would say."[18] Walking in the evening, alone, White's speaker can hear "mellow sounds from distant copse," "softest flute or reeds harmonic joined"; these are

> Romantic sounds! such is the bliss ye give,
>   That heaven's bright scenes seem bursting on the soul,
> With joy I'd yield each sensual wish, to live
>   For ever 'neath your undefiled control. (ll. 29-32)

This is the music of beauty, even when it makes one feel "that heaven's bright scenes seem bursting on the soul," but it is only bringing the listener to the threshold of the sublime, into which he cannot pass unless indeed he could "yield each sensual wish." This is an aesthetic anxiety of greater importance than the kind that Collins expresses in his ode on "The Passions." White himself knows the power of music to tease one out of the form itself, while Collins can only speculate that once upon a time and for others music could be as powerful as it is reputed once to have been. White, even though he was only a youngster of fourteen or fifteen when he composed "Music," was more alive than was William Collins to the significance of music for poetry, Milton's "Sphear-born harmonious Sisters."

His youthful anxiety is expressed by his line of longing: "With her in pensive mood I long to roam" (l. 17); also, in his willingness to yield his fleshly being, *if he could:* "With joy I'd yield each sensual wish." In these touches, slight though deft, White anticipates the Keats of such poems as his "Ode to a Nightingale." But the final quatrain, a kind of coda for the rest of the poem, is far less able, more typically White imitating eighteenth-century sentiment and the style of sensibility:

> Oh! surely melody from heaven was sent,
>   To cheer the soul when tired with human strife,
> To soothe the wayward heart by sorrow rent,
>   And soften down the rugged road of life. (ll. 33-36)

It may be expressed as a function of the poet's longing more than of his firm belief (signaled by the word "surely"), but it is a thought that aptly summarizes those virtues of music which make it an art of the beautiful: it can *"cheer* the soul," *"soothe* the wayward heart," and *"soften . . . life."* None of these effects takes one far out of the comfort of contentment with his human being, with his place in the larger scheme of natural being. They make one feel as though earth is his rightful home—a feeling that may even be hostile to sublimity.

CHAPTER 5

In the Tradition of the Sublime: Poetry for the Mind

THROUGHOUT the eighteenth century, men of letters sought for ways to employ the philosophy of John Locke to satisfy their needs to understand themselves and the world around them, as well as the world beyond them. For the most part, they built upon Locke's famous principle that all knowledge derives from *experience*, that what we call "mind" is a product of sensation and reflection. Whether it was philosophy or poetry, understanding had to begin with Locke's position; philosophers of aesthetics and ethics, from Berkeley to Hartley to Burke, sought to connect mind with matter, or mind with mind; and the poets, from Pope to Akenside to Wordsworth, followed suit.[1] Poetry was increasingly conscious of itself as an art that could make these connections between sight, sound, and mind. While painting could best appeal to the sensation of sight, and music to sound, only poetry could combine both in an appeal to mind itself, that to which all experience leads or to which it ultimately must refer. "Burke himself had urged simply that words produce three effects in the mind of the hearer—the sound, the picture, and the affection of soul produced by either or both the foregoing. . . . Words, indeed, may affect us even more strongly than the things they represent."[2] Poetry which brings the self home to itself, lifts the mind above the mix of matter from which it derives, and celebrates the powers of mind as the unique achievement of God and Nature—that is poetry of the sublime.

When Kirke White wanted to illustrate for his brother what he meant by the sublime, he chose a passage from each of two poems he considered to be major achievements of eighteenth-century literature: "The Pleasures of Melancholy" (1747), by Thomas Warton, the Younger, and *The Pleasures of Imagination*

(1744, 1770), by Mark Akenside. In his letter to his brother, White says that "Warton is a poet from whom I have derived the most exquisite pleasure and gratification. He abounds in sublimity and loftiness of thought"; then he goes on to cite a passage from "The Pleasure of Melancholy" that he admires for its sublimity:[3]

> Nor undelightful is the solemn noon
> Of night, when, haply, wakeful from my couch
> I start: lo, all is motionless around!
> Roars not the rushing wind; the sons of men
> And every beast in mute oblivion lie;
> All nature's hush'd in silence and in sleep.
> Oh, then how fearful is it to reflect
> That through the still globe's awful solitude,
> No being wakes but me. (ll. 50-58)

This sublime poem by Thomas Warton was a continuing source of inspiration as well as of images and themes, for Kirke White. From it White learned how the "mother of musings, Contemplation sage" could lead one to those "solemn glooms" "where thoughtful Melancholy loves to muse."

Whether he called it "contemplation," "thought," or "mind," White addressed this power in himself as a means of reaching heights of vision that he knew by the names of "melancholy" or even "imagination." The sublime experience breaks through forms of natural restraint beyond the boundaries of sensation, and so it is often characterized by negation (as in the passage White cites from Warton's poem) or by a catalog of sensations from the vast bounty of nature. The passage White uses from Akenside is an example of the latter: "The high-born soul"

>   springs aloft
> Through fields of air; pursues the flying storm;
> Rides on the vollied lightnings through the heavens;
> Or, yok'd with whirlwinds and the northern blast,
> Sweeps the long tract of day. (I, ll. 186-90)

The catalog is limited only by the potential of the mind itself, for by its capacity to accumulate experiences of height, depth, and breadth, the mind discovers its essentially transcendental power.

And so Akenside's poem shows how the mind rises to such heights:

> Through all the ascent of things enlarge her view,
> Till every bound at length should disappear,
> And infinite perfection close the scene.
>   Call now to mind what high capacious powers
> Lie folded up in man. . . . (I, ll. 219-23)

Edmund Burke analyzed this experience of the sublime in his famous and influential *Enquiry into the Origin of Our Ideas of the Sublime and Beautiful* (1757), which, as we have already seen, Kirke White read and appreciated.[4] Burke's thesis was that the sublime is recognized by a mental state of "astonishment," in which the mind is "robbed of all its powers of acting and reasoning" (p. 57). The crucial point here is that even though a robbery is occurring, those powers being taken away are "acting and reasoning," leaving the dominant one of "terror," or lesser ones of "admiration, reverence and respect." To rob the mind of its pride in reasoning or making ("acting") is exactly what the poets of Sensibility and later Romanticism wanted to accomplish through their art. For White, as for Warton and Akenside, astonishment, admiration, reverence, and respect are the mental states they hope to create in the sublime mode. Their ways of doing this are ways that Burke catalogs in his *Enquiry:* through images of danger and power, such as obscurity and darkness, privation, vastness, and infinity. As we shall see, White readily adopted such images for his graveyard poetry, where the danger and privation of death arouse terror; for his poems of contemplation and melancholy, where danger as privation dominates to drive one from terror to reverence; and for his poetry of Christian triumph, where images of power, the vast and infinite, dominate to fill the mind with astonishment and admiration.

I *Graveyard Poetry: Solemn Vigils of Thought*

One side of White's imagination always saw nature as a vast graveyard, even when another side insisted on celebrating its loveliness and life. He often "asserts his Christian humanity by imagining natural landscape as . . . a 'monitor' of his own death," as Laurence Goldstein has described one of the motives of the "graveyard writers." "If he were to yield to an aesthetic experience of nature he would sacrifice his highest pleasure, the ecstatic vision of eternity's interpenetration into time."[5] We can see this tension between the two sides of White's imagination at work in a fragment of a poem that White began in imitation of James Thomson, specifically of Thomson's "Winter," lines 276-321.[6] In this passage, Thomson describes the pathetic death of a man lost in a snowstorm: "In his own loose-revolving fields the swain / Disastered stands. . . . / In vain for him the officious wife prepares / The fire fair-blazing and the vestment warm" (ll. 278-79, 311-12). The most interesting feature of White's fragment (p. 82) is his refusal to let the swain die in the storm:

> Shivering and blue, the peasant eyes askance
> The drifted fleeces that around him dance,
> And hurries on his half-averted form,
> Stemming the fury of the sidelong storm.
> Him soon shall greet his snow-topped cot of thatch,
> Soon shall his numbed hand tremble on the latch,
> Soon from his chimney's nook the cheerful flame
> Diffuse a genial warmth throughout his flame
> Round the light fire, while roars the north wind loud,
> What merry groups of vacant faces crowd;
> These hail his coming—these his meal prepare,
> And boast in all that cot no lurking care. (ll. 9-20)

Thus, in a poem that begins with the grand, Thomson-like sublime of nature, proceeding to depict a scene of the human caught up in the epic forces of nature, White insists on transforming the pathos into social triumph for the father caught alone in the storm. The fragment is obviously not like Thomson in another respect, that it is in rhyming couplets rather than in blank verse. The regular rhyme adds to the fragment's comforting tone, giving it a closure that suggests security. On each side of this episode of social warmth amidst natural chaos are passages of, first, winter landscape that leaves no place for "Silence" and "Meditation," and, second, a retreat by the speaker to his "own fireside" where he can muse and hope: "Thus fenced and warm, in silent fit, 'tis sweet / To hear without the bitter tempest beat" (ll. 29-30).

From his own comfortable situation, then, the poet can

contemplate the terrors of a winter storm, can enjoy the happy contrast between the wildness of nature and his own warm security. We never fear for the safety of the peasant making his way home, because the speaker cannot believe in the sacrifice of the human by the natural. The mind triumphs over the materialistic; this is a constant feature of Kirke White's poetry in the sublime mode, even when it is set in graveyard scenes. In this same fragment, the poet attempts to open the scene as if it were a vast ground of death: "Loud rage the winds without.—The wintry cloud / O'er the cold northstar casts her flitting shroud." The verse, which shows again that White practices with patterns of assonance and alliteration to represent the sounds he describes, yields the scene to personified ideas ("Silence" and "Meditation"); these in turn yield to the human figure in the landscape, and when the peasant reaches his happy home, the passage yields to the pressure of the poet's own voice. And it is his own situation that the poet really wants to articulate, causing us to realize, in retrospect, that this force of self-expression underlies the entire fragment. When he ends his passage with this couplet, "All, all alone—to sit, and muse, and sigh, / The pensive tenant of obscurity," White has come to the point where he really wants to begin. The contrast between his own loneliness and the domestic happiness of the winter traveler— this is the main point of the poem.

We may hazard the speculation that White cannot take his imitation of Thomson further because White is too Romantic; he is, as Eleanor Sickels has observed about him, "already [in the] high tide of romantic introspection."[7] He is too subjective in his poetic orientation, however much he may attempt to be picturesque or to sing the wonderful harmonies of the natural order. In his more successful, or genuine, graveyard poems, he can be more Romantic in this sense of the subjective, locating the center of reality in his own mind, or spirit, that triumphs over the deadness of matter represented by the forms of the graveyard all about him. Like the speaker of this Thomsonian fragment, White's graveyard speakers are "all, all alone" surrounded only by relics and signs of former life.

His poetry of sublimity is not capable of ecstatic flight, of epic grandeur in the sense that Thomson's could be. White's poetry usually reaches for the sublime through meditation rather than observation, sometimes striving for the distance of a Gray (as in

In the Tradition of the Sublime: Poetry for the Mind

his "Elegy Written in a Country Churchyard") but more often sounding like Parnell, the Wartons, or Young. He attempts to give objectivity to his graveyard meditations in various ways: presenting death as the disease, Consumption, through the victim of the disease; dramatizing these same figures, death, disease, and victim, in an interesting experiment of lyrical drama; and, more typical of the genre, stationing a grieving speaker beside the grave of a beloved.

A fragment beginning "Oh! thou most fatal of Pandora's train" (p. 81) is an address to the disease of Consumption, that most dreaded killer of so many in White's era. This lyric explores, in four rhyming stanzas, the paradoxical character of the dreaded killer. Consumption does not reveal its true nature until it is too late to stop. The first stanza bitterly denounces the silent duplicity of the disease, that cheats its way insidiously into healthy life only to destroy it and its beauty. In fact, it can add to the beauty it will finally destroy: "while thou givest new lustre to the eye, / While o'er the cheek are spread health's ruddy hues, / E'en then life's little rest thy cruel power subdues" (ll. 7-10).

His choice of Consumption as the disease to address may be more than a biographical matter for us to understand about White's graveyard poetry, for this disease that favors youth, conceals its fatal mission beneath misleading signs of health, is a convenient metaphor that White, as poet, can exploit to probe the paradoxical relationships of beauty, love, and death. In this same fragment, after the initial stanza that describes the way Consumption works, the poet quickly moves to describe the kind of victim usually chosen by the disease: "the glow of youth" whose bloom merely forecasts an early entombment in "the cold vault of death." Then, in the final stanzas, the poet focuses on one particular youthful victim, a beautiful girl who, while calmly sinking "in death's repugnant trance," appeared to become more and more beautiful:

> Even then so beauteous did her form appear,
>   That none who saw her but admiring said,
>   Sure so much beauty never could be dead. (25-27)

The intriguing question, which the poet cannot answer here, is why death can be a cause of beauty.

With this question in mind, we can return to the beginning of the poem and see that the lyric gets its force from a matter of thought rather than from a matter of feeling (which might explain why it is only a fragment). In other words, the poem is more of an intellectual puzzle than an expression of emotion. The poet is not deploring the deaths of loved ones so much as he is analyzing a curiosity: the aesthetic of death. He is interested in the fact that Consumption is a "silent cheater of the eye," that it can give "new lustre to the eye" (of the victim), slowly attacks "the liquid lustre of [the] fine blue eye," and leaves a final impression in an "expressive eye." Such a succession of images, variants of the eye, suggests that White's concern is to show how sight deceives, how vision cheats, and how sensuous beauty is a product of this insidious deception. The poet as a maker of beauty must learn to cope with this phenomenon, this "most fatal of Pandora's train," for he also wishes to make beauty.

Such questions about death and beauty are more explicitly raised in the only attempt White made to compose drama, apparently given its title by Southey: "Fragment of an Eccentric Drama" (p. 101). In this piece White does several surprising, and aesthetically pleasing, things, including an opening lyric to accompany a "dance of the consumptives," and a joining of the figures of Consumption and Melancholy. This latter is a surprise for the reader of White's essays on Melancholy, where he made careful attempts to define melancholy as healthy philosophy. In this piece of poetic drama, however, he makes melancholy not only an ally of a dread disease (indeed, they are "sisters"), but he even tells us that Consumption works to "feed" Melancholy. Finally, in the category of surprises, he presents the heroine of the drama, Angelina, as a beautiful victim of these curious sisters, a victim for whom "the coffin must be her bridal bed" (l. 87). The surprise is that here White explicitly yokes sexual love with death and beauty.

White's "eccentric drama" has, then, some very interesting aesthetic features, sometimes mature in form as well as in thought. To begin with, the drama opens with a haunting song of the dead:

> Ding-Dong! ding-dong!
>   Merry, merry, go the bells,
> Ding-dong! ding-dong!

> Over the heath, over the moor, and over the dale,
> 'Swinging slow with sullen roar,'
> Ding-dong, ding-dong calls us away. (ll. 1-6)

Through three such stanzas we are introduced to a dance of the consumptives, the ghostly dead who dance their way into their "death-beds bleak, / Where the green sod grows upon the grave." This *danse macabre* is darkly ironic, echoing Jacobean tragedy or anticipating in some respects the strange dramas of Beddoes. We are invited to imagine these consumptive figures dancing "merrily" through the darkness of night, ending their festivity only with the dawning of the new day. As "consumptives," they would ordinarily still be alive, slowly dancing their ways to death, but White presents them as already dead, though not so dead that they cannot give some continuing appearance of being alive. We should not miss the important point that they make the music we hear when the drama opens. It is indeed a worthy beginning for a youngster; as Southey says in a note to the drama, "there is something strikingly wild and original in this Fragment" (p. 101).

As the death bells fade away into the early morning hours and the consumptives seek out their deathbeds, out of the sky comes "the Goddess of Consumption, habited in a sky-blue robe, attended by mournful music." She calls for her sister Melancholy to join her in this graveyard scene of moonlit darkness. "The Goddess of Melancholy advances out of a deep glen in the rear, habited in black, and covered with a thick veil." These sisters of the night have been called forth by the dance of the consumptives, but they are more interested in maintaining themselves than in the entertainment that summoned them. Melancholy tells her sister that she will "smooth the way for" Consumption who, in turn, will "furnish food" for Melancholy. The major effect of their joint functions will be to cause the death of youthful beauty: "And the grass shall wave / O'er many a grave, / Where youth and beauty sleep together."

This scene shows how conscious the poet is that a certain kind of beauty is the result of a strange, if not morbid, cooperation between disease and melancholy. Melancholy, in this context, prepares the way for Consumption to do its work, a work that in its turn feeds the melancholy state of mind. It seems like an endless cycle, one that is not broken in the drama itself. White knows the important relationship of the state of mind he called melancholy with the contemplation of death and decay, and he knows that it thrives on sensuous beauty as indeed the beauty may itself thrive on them; however, what remains unclear is how conscious White is that all of this is somehow related to "disease," even though he clearly uses a disease as a main character.

These two goddesses note the arrival of a beautiful young woman, Angelina, drawn to this dark spot by a pale moon whose light she has been following through the night. Consumption vows to possess her:

> She is mine, and I must have her!
> The coffin must be her bridal bed;
> The winding-sheet must wrap her head;
> The whispering winds must o'er her sigh,
> For soon in the grave the maid must lie:
>   The worm it will riot
>   On heavenly diet,
> When death has deflowered her eye. (ll. 86-93)

Remembering that Melancholy has prepared the way and will be fed by this lovely victim, we realize that White is exploring a very complicated issue for himself. And when he adds the element of sexuality to his issue, he has done nothing to simplify it.

It would be easy to overstate the importance of sex to the themes that White explores in his graveyard poetry, for we may be too sensitive to the evidence, given our age's usual orientation to such matters. However, the evidence is present in White's poems of this genre, and it may tell us something about the motives and nature of the genre itself, a matter of more importance than realizing that White was himself merely giving versified expression of his own adolescent yearnings. What graveyard poetry did was to bring together a great many themes that had become clichés, such as the sexual pun on death, with important new anxieties for the writers of the second half of the eighteenth century. These anxieties were fundamentally the consequences of a weakening faith in imagination, in spiritual reality, and so of course the prospect of death posed an even more critical threat than it ever had before.

When love itself, the most impressive evidence of spiritual reality, can lead so easily to death, can become food for melancholy, then it may provide the main clue to the meaning of life confronted by death. Love feeds melancholy—in this drama, at least—because it is *disappointed* love, the figurative parallel for death as the disappointment of life. The drama ends with a long monologue by the heroine, Angelina, who has been marked for death by Melancholy and Consumption. From her speech we learn that she has become vulnerable because she has "felt the pangs of hopeless love." We may read her speech as a lyrical expression of the poet's own self, or we may read it as the development of a character for further dramatic action, or we may read it as White's continuing examination of life's paradoxes.

Angelina's monologue (ll. 94-164), which ends the fragment, contains some of Kirke White's most imaginative and vigorous poetry: imaginative because of its abundant imagery and figurative language, and vigorous because of its confident, uninterrupted rhythm. It tells us what White could have done had he pursued his poetic career further.

> With what a silent and dejected pace
> Dost thou, wan Moon! upon thy way advance
> In the blue welkin's vault!—Pale wanderer!
> Hast thou too felt the pangs of hopeless love,
> That thus, with such a melancholy grace,
> Thou dost pursue thy solitary course?
> . . . .
>   Wan traveller,
> How like thy fate to mine!—Yet I have still
> One heavenly hope remaining, which thou lack'st;
> My woes will soon be buried in the grave
> Of kind forgetfulness—my journey here,
> Though it be darksome, joyless, and forlorn,
> Is yet but short, and soon my weary feet
> Will greet the peaceful inn of lasting rest.
> But thou, unhappy Queen! art doomed to trace
> Thy lonely walk in the drear realms of night.
>   (ll. 94-99, 105-14)

Reading the speech as an expression of the poet's own thought and feeling, we hear little that is new even though we hear it in what is perhaps a more skillful medium. Themes of solitude, life as a journey, life as a summary of trifles, of disappointments and disregard by others—these are the main themes we have come to expect from White's other poetry. Although he adds that rare theme (for him) of unrequited love, even this seems related to his larger concern that all life has turned its back on his claim for fame, has refused to encourage his talent with applause and financial support. That the speech belongs to a girl may suggest that White is masking his own feeling, or imagining the feeling of someone he may himself have unsuccessfully wooed (a defensive reaction), or a dramatization of beauty as female sentiment. As a character in her own right, Angelina does not develop because the drama is not continued beyond her monologue.

Looking, finally, at this monologue as a continuation by White of his "philosophical" meditation on the meaning of life, we may be more impressed with the richness of life it describes than we are by the mysteries of death. When she describes the Moon as a lover disappointed by the departure of her lover Endymion, Angelina is projecting upon the moon a fancy of her own life's situation, suggesting that she has either been sexually loved and deserted or that she wishes she might be sexually loved as was Cynthia by Endymion. Angelina asks,

> Has thy Endymion, smooth-faced boy, forsook
> The widowed breast—on which the spoiler oft
> Has nestled fondly, while the silver clouds
> Fantastic pillowed thee, and the dim night,
> Obsequious to thy will, encurtained round
> With its thick fringe thy couch? (ll. 100-105)

All of the sky, in its blue of night ("the blue welkin's vault"), is imagined richly as a curtained bed for lovers. When Angelina goes on to say that her own unhappiness can be ended by death, as Cynthia's cannot, Angelina makes a quick transition to identify the grave as yet another version of a bed: "My woes will soon be buried in the grave . . . [a place] of lasting rest" (ll. 108, 112). In both love and death there is a profound unconsciousness, a vast forgetfulness that reckons high in the scale of value for human experience.

What Angelina most needs at this point is rest, the perfect rest of unconsciousness that death promises:

In the Tradition of the Sublime: Poetry for the Mind

> I shall lay my head,
> My weary aching head, on its last rest,
> And on my lowly bed the grass-green sod,
> Will flourish sweetly. . . .
> . . . .
> . . . Why, I shall sleep so sweetly,
> Laid in my darksome grave, that they themselves
> Might envy me the rest! (ll. 129-32, 137-39)

The bliss of death is its utter release of self from anxiety, from life's "trifling." But Angelina does not want death to be a nothingness, for she goes on to imagine the warm interiors of the homes she leaves behind, with winter scenes of healthy life in process, and even when those she leaves behind will die, they will join her in death as a "happy family": "Where I shall lie, my friends will lay them down, / And dwell with me, a happy family." Death is imagined as a release from anxiety, but not from the happinesses of life. Beauty, then, is a perfection of happy form, and death is a force of perfection for the imagination of melancholy.

We should not demand too much from White as philosopher, and if we do not we can better enjoy the apprentice artist. In this fragment of a drama we can detect a certain flexing of his aesthetic muscle, even a grace of form that promises much more than it contains. It is a virtuoso piece, employing several verse kinds, sound patterns, personifications, allegory, and dramatic monologue; as such it is more interesting than most of the graveyard poetry of the entire century out of which it derives. It is also the most interesting effort made by White himself in this genre. It shows progress in his imaginative growth and technical improvement, even though it does not take him much closer to a philosophical resolution of his metaphysical puzzles.

Graveyard vigils are occasions, in the eighteenth-century genre, for sublimity, just as the vast expanse of nature had been for Thomson and his followers. For the latter, to comprehend the fullness of the creation was an expansion of the imagination into the sublime; for the graveyard poets, to comprehend the nothingness of death's destruction was also an expansion into the sublime. The one way might be compared with the *via naturaliter positiva* of mysticism, and the other with the *via naturaliter negativa.* For this negative way, death is a great blank upon which the poet can project, unchallenged, the forms of his own fancy. As an experience of the sublime, it is the nothingness that dazzles with its infinitude of possibilities.

Angelina's monologue has a pattern for the sublime experience that we can find in most poems of this kind; she yearns for something beyond the disappointments of life, she imagines the grave as a bed of rest, of forgetfulness, and then she, vigorously, imagines the lives of those she must leave behind until they join her in the "happy family" of death. When she equates her bed of death with the bed of love, Angelina is making an imaginative projection of desire upon death's great blankness, and her resulting thoughts of happy domesticity are the fruit of her sublime experience: a confirmation of her self as a value, as worthy of human happiness.

In his "Lines Supposed to Be Spoken by a Lover at the Grave of His Mistress" (p. 68), White reverses the situation of Angelina, or put in another way, shows us a repentant lover now mourning his beloved over her grave. It is a nicely typical poem for showing just how well White can compose graveyard poetry, giving it special turns that make it individual as well as typical. Such poems, which summon the return of the dead through some kind of ritual process, are at least as old as Homer's *Odyssey*, where (in Book XI) Odysseus summons the shades of the dead to drink the blood he has just poured upon specially prepared ground, or they are as recent as Macpherson's "Ossianic" poems that invoke endless parades of the dead. But White's poem is modest by comparison with Homer or Macpherson, for it simply pictures the bereaved lover who wishes to communicate with his beloved, not to learn how to become heroic or prepare himself for a hero's death.

In fifty-three lines of blank verse, White's speaker calls for his dead lover to confirm a vision he once had of her return during a storm:

>   Come, as thou didst,
> When o'er the barren moors the night wind howled,
> And the deep thunders shook the ebon throne
> Of the startled night!—Oh! then, as lone reclining,
> I listened sadly to the dismal storm,
> Thou, on the lambent lightnings wild careering
> Didst strike my moody eye; (ll. 9-15)

That visionary experience of sublime transport during a "dismal storm" he would like to repeat now during a night of calm stillness, during a "solemn night": "Spirit of her! / My only love! Oh! now again arise" (ll. 22-23).

But his call goes unanswered. At the point where Edward completes his invocation, White turns a nice trick of imagination, for he turns *Edward* into the ghost whose words fill the still evening: "Now lost he stands, / The ghost of what he was" (ll. 48-49). He becomes what he desires, and in his imagination of their reunion, Edward identifies his death with Mary's death, his body dissolving into her body in a grisly necrophilia:

> Mary, soon
> Thy love will lay his pallid cheek to thine,
> And sweetly will he sleep with thee in death. (ll. 51-53)

On this note White ends his poem, for it is the reward of the sublime experience that one returns from it to an affirmation of his own value. To describe the conclusion as "grisly necrophilia" is not to make a judgment about White or his character Edward; rather, it is to approximate the effect the poet desires, to mix the grisly with the beautiful, the pain with the pleasure, and the living with the dead.

The poet drops the pretense of dramatization in his lines "Written in the Prospect of Death" (p. 78), for here he speaks in his own person, but like Edward in the previous poem, he also anticipates an early death. But White (who names himself in his poem, at line 38) is not involved in a ritual of calling for the return of a dead lover's phantom, as Edward is; instead, the poet calls for something more important to himself—"Thought," "Sad solitary Thought." It is meditation itself, or the state of mind that gives rise to meditation, that he summons "in the prospect of death." And by "thought" White means "understanding," an explanation for death as a rational conclusion to a life that has accomplished so little. The poem is a kind of "complaint" (to use the term that Young had used for his *Night Thoughts*) searching for "consolation."

There is much more complaint than there is consolation. After fifty-one lines of complaint, the poet resigns himself to his death, surrenders his hopes and ambitions, to prepare himself for the reward of heaven:

> I abjure all. Now other cares engross me,
> And my tired soul, with emulative haste,
> Looks to its God, and prunes its wings for heaven. (ll. 55-57)

This concludes the poem, weakly, after some strong lines of emotional force. When he says that he abjures all, he says something strong; even when he says "other cares engross" him, he is still saying something strong, but when he explains those "other cares," the poet comes close to the bitter irony that we sometimes hear in a lyric by William Blake: for, to prune one's wings, for heaven or anything else, is a painful prospect of diminishment, not enlargement and reward.

Perhaps we should not make so much of this conventional ending, but as the end of a long meditation that deplores the prospect of death, it could not carry much conviction on its own. The "thought" which the poet calls for turns out to be an anxiety, perhaps melancholy itself. It does not deliver much consolation, as we have seen, but it does create visions of sublime terror. The entire experience turns on a major irony: that the speaker cannot sleep at this midnight hour because he is afraid of death, the big sleep. In this examination of his own mind, this communing with "Thought," the poet discovers an essential blankness, a nothingness at the heart of his being, and this it is that strikes fear into him:

> Yet do I feel my soul recoil within me
> As I contemplate the dim gulf of death,
> The shuddering void, the awful blank—futurity. (ll. 28-30)

Life conceived as a time glass with "fleeting particles" falling into nothingness, "silent, unseen, unnoticed, unlamented," or as a binding together of such particles, only to be cut apart by the knife of death: such a conception of life is fundamentally materialistic, atomistic, and so the poet's only real hope for meaning is that "thought" or mind can survive the "pruning" of Death's heavy hand.

Images of falling, sinking, dissolving into blankness give this poem a richness often missing from the texture of White's poetry. All of these images gather to a strong crisis in the following lines:

> I shall sink
> As sinks a stranger in the crowded streets

> Of busy London: —some short bustle's caused,
> A few inquiries, and the crowds close in,
> And all's forgotten. (ll. 41-45)

The simile works to dramatize the horror of death as the ultimate experience of anonymity, the horror of most people's everyday life in a world filled with faceless crowds. This horror is akin to another, "the powerful fear of being orphaned by God, of being exiled in the flesh," which Laurence Goldstein identifies as an important motive for "graveyard literature."[8] The horror of anonymity works in two directions for White's poem: it points us toward the annihilation of identity that death threatens, but it also points us back to the poet's own anxiety that his reputation as an artist will not survive his death. The poem is, finally, a cry for recognition even as it submits itself to "the gaping gulf of blank oblivion."

This same theme of public recognition to prevent anonymity lies behind White's "Lines Written in Wilford Churchyard" (p. 127), which echoes Gray's poem not only in the title but also in the line, "Such a one perchance did Gray, Frequent" (ll. 10-11). But, despite this conscious echoing of Gray, White's poem has little more in common with the celebrated "Elegy" than the graveyard situation and the speaker who imagines himself lying among the dead whose graves he observes; indeed, whereas Gray's poem makes its famous transition to put the speaker among the dead at the end of the "Elegy," White's poem is throughout a meditation on the speaker's own death and final resting place. It is as though White had taken only the last section of Gray's poem for imitation.[9]

Behind Gray's poem was Thomas Parnell's "Night-Piece on Death" (1721), a poem which makes a point of death as "a port of calms, a state of ease" (l. 69), and so it is an influence of considerable importance for White's poem, with its continuous theme of rest and sleep among the dead.[10] Another looming presence in White's poem is Robert Blair's famous blank-verse meditation on "the Grave." Blair's poem is much more sententious than White's, however (as indeed is Gray's). Probably White's disgust with the "rude sexton" (l. 47) is a conscious borrowing from Blair's long passage on the sottish sexton (ll. 452-66 of "The Grave").[11] As a final note on conscious imitation, we should notice that White's focus on the decaying corpse, with its "moist flesh" and "tenacious hair" (ll. 49, 50), partakes of the same gruesome interest so abundant in James Hervey's very popular *Meditations among the Tombs* (1746-47); Hervey's "religious dread" prompts him to explore tombs in grisly detail.[12] But White has little more than the two lines already quoted to describe decaying corpses, for this is not his real interest any more than it is his intent to moralize in the manner of Blair or Gray.

White, unlike all these predecessors, is interested in himself as the main subject of his graveyard meditation. Coincidentally, his poem is unlike the works of Parnell, Blair, Hervey, and Gray in its daytime setting, when "the sultry sun, / From his meridian height, endeavours vainly / To pierce the shadowy foliage" (ll. 5-7). These "lines written in Wilford Churchyard" show a Wordsworthian fixation with place, a spot where the spirit can locate itself: "This is the spot," "It is a lovely spot," "in this same spot," he hopes for relief for his "harrassed soul" (ll. 2, 6, 16). The tone is wistful, wishful, without enthusiasm; it is made speculative by the poet's desire to stop his wandering, belabored spirit and fix it in same permanent repose without the heavy burden of this weary world laid upon it.

Death is a shading from life's harsh sunlight; it is a "pleasant nook" like the one where the speaker stops to rest. The poem has a poignancy that comes from the main theme of hope for rest, something that would appeal to a laboring class of people who would become the main audience for literature in the nineteenth century. White's poem is a yearning not for the nothingness of death (usually he is afraid of that "blank oblivion"), but rather for a release from the harassment of life's drudgery and pettiness. The poem's main texture is a pattern of contrasts, all designed to reenforce the theme of tension between the weariness of the traveler and his yearning for rest. The "sultry sun" endeavors "vainly / To pierce the shadowy foliage"; the "corpse cemented down / With brick and stone" is contrasted with the light rest of one buried "beneath a little hillock, a grass o'er grown, / Swathed down with osiers" (ll. 22-23); the harsh conditions of urban graveyards are contrasted with the respectfully tender conditions of rural graveyards (ll. 45-66). All of these contrasts imply a scheme of values that mark White as well as his era, moving as it is from a rural to an urban culture and so contrasting its past of peace with its present of "wanton havoc" (l. 66).

To "wanton" is not in itself bad for White in this poem, but the playfulness of the wanton must be innocent if not creative. In the opening of the poem, White characterizes Gray's having written his "Elegy" in a "wanton" mood: "Such a one perchance did Gray / Frequent, as with a vagrant muse he wantoned" (ll. 10-11). The notion of playfulness was strong in the poet's mind, for he felt that the refreshing breeze was playing about his cheek: "the zephyr / Comes wafting gently o'er the rippling Trent / And plays about my wan cheek" (ll. 7-9). It is as though White uses the metaphor of play to suggest that his art, as the vehicle of his fancy, provides a release (his "longed release," l. 79) from the harsh restraints of a world that otherwise lacks respect for genius and turns play into havoc. Like Gray, then, White "wantons" with a muse in a country setting, or rather in the pastoral elegy, where such play can still be creative.

What is created by such play of the imagination is an ideal of self-satisfaction and spiritual freedom. Moving back and forth between the harsh sunlight and the cool shade, between the cool river and the hot summer road, between the brick and stone tomb to the grassy hillock, between the disrespectful city sexton and the respectful rustic laborer, the poet's mind generates a spirit of imagination that achieves sublimity in its desires:

> Grant, Heaven, that here my pilgrimage may close!
> Yet, if this be denied, where'er my bones
> May lie—or in the city's crowded bounds,
> Or scattered wide o'er the huge sweep of waters,
> Or left prey on some deserted shore
> To the rapacious cormorant,—yet still
> (For why should sober reason cast away
> A thought which soothes the soul?) yet still my spirit
> Shall wing its way to these my native regions,
> And hover o'er this spot. (ll. 67-76)

The passage echoes not only the Wordsworthian mood of "Tintern Abbey," but it even sounds like Wordsworth in its reluctance to accept fully the largeness of vision that opens out to it; rather, it must overcome the restraint of "sober reason" to assert its spiritual freedom signified by this "lovely spot."

Spiritual freedom turns out to be a condition for earthly happiness, in a finer tone, stripped of its wretchedness and pains, described as the final reward of death in the companion poems

"Thanatos" (p. 116) and "Athanatos" (p. 117). These are, in the manner of Milton's "L'Allegro" and "Il Penseroso," examinations of different prospects, not vocations of life as in Milton's poems, but rather vocations of death. Even though "Athanatos" suggests by its title that it is "against death" or is "deathless," that is only a figurative way to deny a particular attitude or conception of death, not a denial that death is inevitable. "Thanatos" contrasts, again as in many of White's poems, the heavy weight of this life with the apparent ease of death: "who would cherish life, And cling unto this heavy clog of clay" (ll. 1-2); "welcome, oh! thou silent maid, / Who in some foggy vault art laid," and "Death is the best, the only cure" (ll. 13-14, 25-26). What death has to offer, from this point of view, is complete rest, utter stasis with all its security of permanence: "all thy senses stupified / Are to marble petrified" (ll. 19-20). "Thanatos" promises "the Gothic Tomb," "a stately monument," and "the harmonious thunders" of "the pealing organ." The result will be a sweet sleep "shut out from thoughtful misery."

But White will not give himself to such an ideal of death, an ideal that denies the value of "thought" and conscious being, frozen as it is in cold marble and "mouldering" grandeur. We know, even without the companion piece of "Athanatos" that the poet does not agree with the speaker of "Thanatos," for he gives too many signs of disapproval: "away with life!," "foggy vault," "dismal sway," "unwholesome damps," "stupified," and many other phrases signal White's own disagreement. That kind of celebration of death is "unwholesome" just to the extent that it denies all the good that there is in life, with its "vital fire," as he puts it in "Athanatos" (l. 7).

This companion poem is not an unwholesome denial of life, but it is an indictment of life's storms and sorrows. What it calls "the calm reality" of "Immortality" sounds very much like simple happiness in this life, where "all the joys which death did sever, / [are] given to us again for ever" (ll. 34-35). The poem confirms what we have always suspected about White's graveyard verse: that he does not celebrate death, indeed he fears its threat of extinction and anonymity; what he does celebrate is the death of imperfection, the death of deceit and strife, as a purification of this life that releases the human spirit to its complete self-assertion. That is what motivates his concluding tone of the sublime in this poem: "When the glorious prospect lies / Full before his raptured eyes."

II *Poems of Contemplation: The Genius of Melancholy*

From Thomas Warton's "Pleasures of Melancholy," a model of the sublime poem for Kirke White, the younger poet took an abundance of themes, settings, images, and phrases which he frequently used in the making of his own poems.[13] It is probably from Warton's poem that White gets the idea of making Contemplation into a figure of the power to inspire sublimity: Wharton's poem opens with an invocation to the "Mother of musings, Contemplation sage," to lead him "to solemn glooms / Congenial with [his] soul" (ll. 1, 17-18). As the "mother of musings," Contemplation is the "queen sublime" for Warton, who goes on to conclude his poem with yet another address to this same figure:

> Then ever, beauteous Contemplation, hail!
> From thee began, auspicious maid, my song,
> With thee shall end. . . . (ll. 300-302)

This is the power that leads the mind to "where thoughtful Melancholy loves to muse" (l. 20).

Kirke White also associates Contemplation with Melancholy, which together lead the mind to "explore / This fleeting state of things" (as Warton's poem puts it, ll. 80-81). While "The Pleasures of Melancholy" emphasizes "the spoils / Of sunk magnificence" for achieving the "loftier rapture" (ll. 275-76, 304), White's poetry of the sublime pleasures of melancholy is more likely to emphasize the "viewless boundaries" of "truths sublime" (as in the poem from which these phrases come, "Lines Written on a Survey of the Heavens," p. 65). The objects of sublimity for White's poetry are without clear definition; indeed, they are *viewless* in the same sense that space is boundless, and as we shall see later, this lack of focus is an essential feature of the sublime experience for White, as indeed it is for most art of the sublime, according to Edmund Burke in his *Enquiry*.

White is more interested in the *power* of sublime vision than he is in the contents of that vision. He tends to identify this power as a pure act of mind, an act which unites the mind of man with God as Pure Mind. Martin Price, commenting on the importance of critics in the Platonic tradition of the sublime, explains their stress on "the oneness of the human and the divine. . . . The transcendence which the sublime reveals is that moment when man feels most acutely in himself the divine principle that governs the cosmos."[14] Hence, the sublime is the height of human rapture. White's sublime experience does not, then, search out mouldering ruins so much as it tries to rise above them, realizing that all earth is but such a ruin that must be transcended. Earth's attractions are for White's visionary a force of restraint, sometimes strong, upon his desire for the sublime.

In his poem "To Contemplation" (p. 122), White gives thanks to Contemplation as a power of imagination to rescue him from the life of common things. In this blank verse of sixty-two lines, he begins in a conversational tone that passes from the apologetic to the strident and ends on a vigorous note of self-assertion. Because of his power of Contemplation, he has been blamed and censured by others who think he cannot attend to practical matters, because he will not "tie [His] every thought down to the desk, and spend / The morning of [his] life adding figures" (ll. 4-5). From such drudgery his is a daydreamer's life, filled with "vagrant thoughts" that turn him into "a wayward youth, misled by Fancy's vagaries" (ll. 14, 24).

The "monotony" of "money getting" is a human ruin from which Contemplation rescues him, for this power awakens his "mind's eye" and sends his "thoughts ten thousand leagues away" in experiences that make his "opening mind" both "ductile" and "plastic." In this poem White is satisfied if he can ride this power away from "the dusky track of commerce," enjoy "the wings of Fancy," and "partake of happiness on earth" (ll. 55, 59, 60). There is no thought of rising above the earth to join with God, for "to be happy here is man's chief end" (l. 61). The main theme and emphasis of the lines "To Contemplation" is on the liberating power of thought, of "meditation" to distinguish the self from "the busy bustling crowds." In this poem, White emphasizes "the subject's struggle to become adequate to its object," as Martin Price describes the dynamics of a sublime poem; "characteristically," he goes on to say, "we move from the mind's struggle to become adequate to the divine to the mind's inherent divinity shedding the objects that limit its powers."[15]

"To Contemplation" is formed mostly in the past tense,

however, and the poet addresses his cherished power as something he learned to value when he was young, before "growing years / Had . . . taught [him] man was made to mourn" (ll. 39-40). This fact of man's sorrow is a matter of increasing concern in White's poetry, as he strives to organize his values into a coherence of some kind. The sorrow, of melancholy, will eventually teach him that all nature, not only the dust and monotony of it, must be escaped by means of the very same power he first learned to love as contemplation. The process of this education is the subject of one of White's longest poems, unfinished, that he called simply "Childhood" (p. 37). It is composed in rhyming couplets of 420 lines, and it is divided into two parts. Part I, made up of 159 lines, describes childhood experiences in a village grammar school where the speaker's talent was first discovered and nourished by the attentions of a matron, "gentle of heart, yet knowing well to rule" (l. 44). Part II, made up of the balance of the poem, concentrates on a friendship he formed while attending "the public school" to which he was "compelled to go" (l. 196).

This long poem is a nostalgic look back "in memory's mellowing glass" where the poet roams "in fancy in each cherished scene" (ll. 1, 3). In those "unclouded skies of former days" he remembers best his joys in "the village churchyard, and the village green." The primary focus on the churchyard is an interesting feature, telling us not only something about the ordinary life of the village that is centered around the church and the graveyard, but also telling us that life was quickly associated with death in such a culture. It was, however, not death associated with separation and sorrow, at least not for this youngster. The churchyard was a place of play and sport, as remembered through this "mellowing glass." After describing further the kindly but stern practices of his schoolteacher, White explains a main motive for his poem, that it allows him an escape from "life's alarms":

> Childhood, to thee I turn, from life's alarms,
> Serenest season of perpetual calms,—
> Turn with delight, and bid the passions cease,—
> And joy to think with thee I tasted peace. (ll. 90-93)

Composing the poem is itself a peaceful experience, and his memories of childhood put into play the power he discovered and developed in that very childhood: "then 'twas first I caught / The first foundation of romantic thought" (ll. 146-47). The particular reference here is to hearing stories and songs from his teacher (ll. 130-45), and so it was her storytelling that was most valuable to this budding poet: "She told of innocence foredoomed to bleed, / Of wicked guardians bent on bloody deed," but it was not the content of her tales that uplifted the boy—it was the "wonder" she aroused in him, a power to "soar on the wings of fancy through the air, / To realms of light, and pierce the radiance there," as the poet feels what he describes while ending the first part of his poem (ll. 158-59).

To "soar" "to realms of light, and pierce the radiance there" prefigures the experience of the sublime, if it is not the sublime itself. Before the imagination can be conscious of itself as a power of the sublime, it will have to know the force of sorrow, or "the pleasures of melancholy," if that paradoxical way of putting it is acceptable. Part II takes the poet a step in that direction, for it narrates his introduction to the darker world that lay before him by way of the "public school," where "the dark deformities of man [began to] appear" (l. 203). Amidst the darker scene he found out a new value, marking his growth in maturity; he found there the value of friendship, and tells how he enjoyed his life with a certain fellow student named George. The melancholy association with George is not only a matter of now-long separation from him as a colleague of the distant past, but it is more profoundly an utter separation by death. His memory's picture of George is therefore tinged with sorrow as he surveys his friend "in life's dismaying road" (l. 235).

Death removed his friend from life, but the poet's own memory and imagination rescue the value of the friendship as something that cannot die. Suddenly, he hears a familiar voice in the breeze: "Yes! yes! his spirit's near!—The whispering breeze / Conveys his voice sad sighing on the trees" (ll. 240-41). This marks the poet's recovery of spirit in "Fancy's wild aerial dream" whose "fond illusions" bear the form of new life even as they contain "fond" images of the past ("fond" in the sense of both *dear* and *foolish*). Remembering the dead friend recalls days of happiness in his company. The next hundred lines of the poem narrate a typical day's adventure, in which the boys would rise early to enjoy "reviving Nature" with the "returning day," soaring in vision with the lark as it rose and rose "till the pained sight no more / Could trace him in his high aerial tour" (ll. 294-95); such an experience was a basis for the young poet's own pattern of imaginative ascent, rising as it does from forms of sight to forms of sound and then beyond to boundlessness.

The poet knows the value of such experiences, and after he goes on to describe other events of such a day's ramble for boys, he celebrates what he has retained:

> Yet even then, (for oh! what chains can bind,
> What powers control, the energies of mind!)
> E'en then we soared to many a height sublime. (ll. 332-34)

The word "sublime," or some variant, is more and more frequently used as White draws near the conclusion of this second part, and in this poem he makes a conscious association with divinity: "All, all was pregnant with divine delight" in those glorious days. But now, in the present, after intervening years of sorrow and pain, the poet must bring his childhood song to a close ("That song must close," he says sorrowfully in line 399, and repeats again at line 403). What he retains is the same power to soar, but now chastened, even if "tired" out with life's contrarieties: "And the tired soul, now led to thoughts sublime, / Looks but for rest beyond the bounds of time" (ll. 375-76).

Before looking at some of the poems White wrote as products of sublime "energies of mind," we should pause here to notice one of his "slighter" poems, "A Letter in Hudibrastic Verse" for his brother, entitled "My Study" (p. 70). At any rate, the poem is a nice example of his good humor, as he describes his tiny room with its crazy window:

> A window vainly stuffed about,
> To keep November's breezes out,
> So crazy, that the pains proclaim
> That soon they mean to leave the frame. (ll. 17-20)

As he goes on to list the contents of his room, a list of his "earthly catalogue" (l. 42), he realizes that what he has described is a scene of apparent confusion: "Confusion's self had settled there" (l. 54). He describes the plaster casts he has collected, casts that could pass for any ancient worthy, so long as the faces with beards were named for men and the ones without for women. Out of this "confusion" emerges in the end a type of order, an order imposed by the organizing power of the poet's mind. The room, with its shoddy, confused mass of trivia, is represented at the end of the poem as but a type of the restraint common life imposes upon "the ideal flights of Madam Brain" (l. 82). And so even this lighthearted little poem about his cramped study becomes an occasion for White to celebrate his "energies of mind" that cannot be contained by any earthly form.

When he was able to devote himself to study in preparation for the ministry, he was troubled by his continuing desire for poetry. On the one hand it would be a diversion from his main calling and the discipline made necessary by that calling, but on the other hand there was in him a lingering instinct for knowing the great value of his art (a self-division that would later torment the much greater poet, Gerard Manley Hopkins). Some of the best moments in White's poetry come while he writes of this self-doubt, and even as he writes he realizes the value of what he thinks he must give up—his art of poetry. In an untitled poem beginning "Yes, my stray steps have wandered" (p. 131), he represents this struggle as a part of his spiritual education in which he must either abandon the poetry or transform it to give it new direction.

The poem opens with an acknowledgment that the poet has "wandered far" from poesy, even though it has powers of soothing the heart. Describing the loveliness of the art, White repeats the idea of "play" with making poetry (ll. 13-16). This playfulness, an abandonment of spirit, was an important part of his art as he understood it, and he knows that it is a sign of vitality, even freedom; but he is troubled by it nevertheless (something that reminds us of his having once flirted with evangelicalism). Poetry is a "sorceress" whose "bonds" he cannot burst (ll. 21-22), but he hears "other duties call" him. Poetry is a "high minstrelsy," but "there are severer strains" with a "sublimer end" than art for its own sake. That "sublimer end" is possible only for those who give themselves to "solemn thought" with its "strange music" that fills "all the soul."

White may not realize it completely in this poem, but his calling is not a simple matter of turning from poetry to religion; it seems more like a calling to solemnize his art, to make what seems to the juvenile a "strange music." The conclusion of the poem is an "arduous path" that leads to "the Queen of Truth," and seems to suggest that the poet will pursue this path at the cost of his art, *but* that is not altogether the case: *"But* for such recollections I *could* brace / My *stubborn* spirit for the arduous path" (ll. 57-58; my italics). The concluding image of "the Queen of Truth" is therefore an ambiguous, if not an ambivalent, one, as the poem hangs upon a tension of "stubborn" refusal to give up the "play" of art for the "arduous" pursuit of "solemn thought." This "Queen of Truth" is probably more of a complex matter than the still immature poet completely realizes. He hopes, without being very comfortable with the hope, he can keep the art with him on his "steep ascent."

With unusually firm control of his material, White makes this same subject the theme of his short poem beginning "If far from me the Fates remove / Domestic peace" (p. 94). In twenty-four lines of octosyllabic couplets, he arranges three sentences that hang from the conditional "if." Behind this "if" is a strong emotion of wistful hope that what he imagines will not be true, that he will *live* to know "domestic peace, connubial love, / The prattling ring, the social cheer" of happiness in this life. But *if* those should be denied him, and we realize he fears that will be the case, *then* he hopes he will have the strength to live with what remains behind for him. The "sterner powers" to which he appeals echo the "severer strains," "solemn thought," and "arduous path" of the poem we have just looked at. This shorter poem presents this social quality as a style of life that may have to compensate for an absence of happier pleasure and softer style.

The alternative of "sterner powers" becomes more attractive as the poem draws to its conclusion, for along the way of truth the poet may "wrap [his] soul in dreams divine / Till earth and care no more be mine" (ll. 15-16). Philosophy will compensate him for the loss of domestic, that is earthly, happiness, so that he may not hear "the prattling ring, the social cheer, / Affection's voice," but he will be able to hear "the music of the spheres" and discover "sublimer lore" (ll. 20, 22).

The best way to strengthen the spirit for an austere endeavor is to learn how to yield the distracting pleasures of life. This is the point of two sonnets in the sublime mode, achieving sublimity through melancholy contemplation. One, "Sweet to the gay of heart is Summer's smile" (p. 190), rejects summer and spring for winter with its "howls of furies" and "melancholy" that "wastes the vital fire." The interesting thing about this poem is its identification of the problem as something like a curse on the poet: he knows the attractions of summer's smile and spring's sweetness (for he is not perverse), but within his soul there rages a howling fury and wasting melancholy that will not let him enjoy such bright scenes: they are in essence untrue to his spiritual truth. The sestet is a yearning to escape the tension of outer happiness contradicted by inner melancholy, but there is no promise that he can make the escape.

Instead, he may have to live with "the anguish of a mental sore, / Which gnaws his heart, and bids him hope no more," as he describes it in the conclusion to his sonnet beginning "Quick o'er the wintry waste dart fiery shafts" (p. 191). This sonnet focuses on a scene of winter gloom where "gaunt Horror stalks" and "the pensive poet 'mid the wild waste walks." He can walk unmindful of the dangers that hover around because he lives within himself more than he lives in the world around him: his thought is his protection. This sonnet reverses the scenes from what they were in the one just examined, where winter within contrasted with summer or spring without. But between the two sonnets we can gather the more important fact that for Kirke White the world he observed was either less real than the one he knew within himself, or it was a world whose reality was fundamentally opposed to the one within, no less real than the one without.

His most extended poem of meditation that leads to sublimity is the "Lines Written on a Survey of the Heavens" (p. 65). White's patron, Capel Lofft, in 1781 "published the longest poem on astronomy of the century and the most prodigious didactic poem on science before Darwin." This poem, entitled *Eudosia: or a Poem on the Universe,* "redeems its mountainous summary of astronomical research with occasional touches of the sublime," according to William Powell Jones.[16] White's poem is certainly not competing with Lofft's except to reach for the sublime by way of a survey of the heavens. He does not set the inner world of spirit in opposition with the outer one of matter as in the two sonnets. It is not anxiety from tension or pain of conflict that motivates this longer poem in blank verse; this poem fixes its gaze on the sky just before dawn, and in that attitude it can disregard any daylight signs of opposition between self and nature.

In the Tradition of the Sublime: Poetry for the Mind

The poem begins with a conventional image of sublimity, "many twinkling stars" filling "the sable vault / Of night's dominions." It will show us how "the wish to be inundated is reversed into a wish to possess."[17] Looking steadily at the scene above, the poet grows increasingly "bewildered" by the scope of thought suggested by this scene "too vast, too boundless for our narrow mind" (l. 9). His own act of meditation generates within him a desire, an energy of mind, to disregard or leap over the appearance of boundaries, and that desire lifts him to an identification with God Himself:

> Thence higher soaring,
> Through ye I raise my solemn thoughts of Him,
> The mighty Founder of this wondrous maze,
> The great Creator! Him! Who now sublime,
> Wrapt in the solitary amplitude
> Of boundless space, above the rolling spheres
> Sits on His silent throne and meditates. (ll. 11-17)

This passage of identification between imagination's energy of desire and "the great Creator" is, for us, a seal of White's instinctual realization of the divine within himself, *as* poet, *as* a "creator" himself. His reaching for adequate images breaks down in such words as "boundless," and "viewless," but it nevertheless marks a threshold for him: he could pass it to concentrate on the imagination itself, that "energy of mind" that both pleases and pains the young man, like his Romantic contemporaries, or he could resign himself to the vague and desperate inability to reach beyond boundaries of experience that characterizes so many of his predecessors in the Age of Sensibility.

III *Religious Musings and Christian Triumphs*

Ten years before Kirke White composed his poem in celebration of "Christmas Day. 1804" (p. 85), Samuel Taylor Coleridge first wrote his poem for the same holiday, "Religious Musings: A Desultory Poem, Written on the Christmas Eve of 1794." Coleridge worked on this poem for the rest of his life and had republished it with some changes only one year before White composed his Christmas poem. The circumstances were right, then, for White to have known about Coleridge's poem, although there is no external evidence to prove it. Certainly, however, it was a fashionable thing to write a birthday poem for Christ, just as Milton had done with his "Ode on the Morning of Christ's Nativity," and so Milton's influence is (not surprisingly) present in both Coleridge's and White's Christmas poems. "Christmas Day. 1804" stands somewhere between the lyrical music of Milton's "Ode" and the prosaic sublimity of Coleridge's "Religious Musings," for White's poem, which opens with lines that echo "Lycidas" (again), is a blank-verse meditation ("musing") rather than a lyrical ode, but it is not stridently ambitious like Coleridge's (which actually imitates the sublime opening of Book III in *Paradise Lost*).

A recent critic has looked at Coleridge's "wildly ambitious poem" that "never stops whooping," and he concludes that even if "Religious Musings" "does seem palpably awful, [y]et its awfulness is at least Sublime."[18] The critic is Harold Bloom, who proceeds to discuss the importance of Coleridge's struggle with the "Miltonic angel."[19] Bloom's theories of influence aside, we can share his own puzzled interest in poetry that may seem palpably awful, yet be fascinated with it as an awfulness that is "at least Sublime." For this is the most striking feature of Kirke White's poems in the sublime mode, particularly the three which are to be discussed in this section: "Christmas Day. 1804," "Time," and *The Christiad*.

Coleridge's "Religious Musings" is a much longer and, being "desultory," a much less coherent poem than White's "Christmas Day."[20] However, each is marked by its main focus on something other than the great religious event of the Incarnation. Coleridge is mainly interested in deploring the world's moral confusion caused by its blindness to the "Supreme Reality" of "God / Diffused through all" (ll. 133, 130-31); the Incarnation was, and *is* for Coleridge, a type of "the Great / Invisible (by symbols only seen)" (ll. 9-10), and his poem becomes an explication of the symbolic presence of the "Great Invisible" throughout the creation. For Coleridge, then, his poem on Christmas is an intellectual analysis of the "Supreme Reality! / The plentitude and permanence of bliss!" He ends his poem with a hope that he may earn the right one day to join the "mystic choir" that breathes "the empyreal air / Of Love, omnific, omnipresent Love" (ll. 410, 414-15).

In the Tradition of the Sublime: Poetry for the Mind

Kirke White also hopes to join in singing "the halleluiahs of the risen God" (l. 49), a hope he expresses in the conclusion to his Christmas poem. The expression of the hope may be conventional, but the choice of images and ideas so differs between Coleridge and White that we realize how various the form can be. Both Coleridge and White are Christian in their religious orientations; Coleridge when he composed his poem was inclining toward the Unitarians, however, and White toward the orthodox Anglicans (although he had been through an evangelical phase). Coleridge's poem emphasizes "Intellectual Love" (as Wordsworth later called it) and the ethical example of Christ as a "symbol" of that love; White's poem emphasizes Christ as "a man of woes" (l. 29) and "the risen God" (l. 49). Strangely, then, both poets leave out of focus the main reason for the occasion: the Incarnation. Coleridge ignores the event as religious history in favor of its ethical symbolism, while White ignores it completely to focus on Christ the Redeemer, on the Resurrection.

Each poem tells us something special about the poet and his uneasy relationship with Christianity; for Coleridge, that relationship was to remain dynamic though increasingly orthodox, and for White, it was always a precarious balance between intellect and feeling, never satisfactorily merged into a coherent whole. "Christmas Day. 1804" repeats White's theme of aspiration to devote himself to new truths; religious discipline might allow him to continue to write poetry, though now "with hymnings high" to answer the call of a "higher quarrel" in such a poem as this, his "loudest song." He does not, like Coleridge, attempt to explain a religious metaphysic or even an ethical philosophy; instead, White contrasts the continuing misery of the world (in lines 15 through 26) with the teachings and life of Christ, who was supposed to "redeem" the world from such misery.

And so it is this contrast that preoccupies the young poet, allowing us to speculate that this is what most moved the young pastor: to relieve human suffering with a message of Christian redemption, of "patience" and "holy fortitude" (ll. 31, 40). White knew all too well the experience of a "soul . . . tossed in troubled seas" (l. 37), and so he easily seized upon the promise of Christ as a liberator of burdened souls, as a comforter of troubled hearts. His own faith was a function of his poetic imagination, something he makes clear in the conclusion of this poem, where he hopes the poem itself may allow him to "join / The halleluiahs of the risen God." Imagining how the "risen God" may accept this poem as a birthday gift, the poet's "grovelling song" becomes a "hymn of faith." In contrast with the conclusion of Coleridge's poem, where the Self of the poet is "annihilated" as it is absorbed into the "Identity" of "God in all," in White's conclusion it is God (Christ) who is taken into the poet's Self: "Lord of life, / The Christ, the Comforter, Thine advent now / Fills my uprising soul" (ll. 54-56).

Here is the real Incarnation for White, when his own imaginative faith raises him to receive the "advent" of Christ; when, in other words, God "fills" the man Kirke White. This was a satisfactory resolution of White's poetic crisis: that in making his poems, he makes gifts for God, but paradoxically the gift-making opens his soul or mind to receive that very God as Himself the gift. The poet filled with God is the divine man who realizes that "by our own spirits are we deified," as Wordsworth put it about the same time (in "Resolution and Independence"). This realization is the force that motivates the sublime conclusion of White's Christmas poem:

> I mount, I fly
> Far o'er the skies, beyond the rolling orbs;
> The bonds of flesh dissolve, and earth recedes,
> And care, and pain, and sorrow are no more.

Although his was a different way of getting there, White's transport of spirit takes him into that same "infinitude" which is "our destiny, our being's heart and home" that Wordsworth described while writing about his disappointment on crossing the Simplon Pass. The year Wordsworth first drafted the passage containing these insights was 1804, and the passage was to be a part of his "poem on the growth of a poet's mind." Wordsworth and White, quite independently of one another, were learning how to say to their "conscious soul," " 'I recognize thy glory' "[21]

Kirke White, like the great Romantic poets, including Coleridge, Wordsworth, and Blake, worked in the long shadow cast by the genius of Milton. Each, in his own way, rewrote Milton's great poetry, as later so would Keats and Shelley. But the Romantic poets only succeeded where their eighteenth-century brethren had failed in trying to rewrite, or imitate, the great epics of Milton. Among the more interesting failures of the century was Edward Young's epic "graveyard" meditation in the sublime mode, *The Complaint: Or, Night Thoughts on Life, Death, and Immortality* (1742).[22] This poem, in nine parts (or "nights"), is composed of more than 9,000 lines of blank verse; it mixes elegiac reflection with Christian apologetic. Each part is spoken by a man meditating late into the night on the themes announced by the subtitle, "life, death, and immortality."

Sometimes the speaker of *Night Thoughts* addresses his arguments toward a certain "Lorenzo," whom the poem is intended to convert from atheism to Christian faith. The speaker uses the examples of persons who recently died to illustrate the points of his discourse; he insists, especially in "Night VII," that life is so filled with pain and horror that without the hope of immortality, man could find no meaning in his existence. The ninth "Night" is the longest and the best part of the poem; it surveys the heavens to demonstrate from the evidence of nature that "all things speak a God" (774). Young celebrates this evidence made available by the new astronomy:

> Devotion! daughter of Astronomy!
> An undevout astronomer is mad.
> True; all things speak a God; but in the small,
> Men trace out Him; in great, He seizes man;
> Seizes, and elevates, and wraps, and fills
> With new inquiries, 'mid associates new. (IX, ll. 772-77)

The person who considers the vast scope of the creation rises toward that religious sublimity which Young and many other writers of the era, including Kirke White, attempt to achieve in their art:

> Nature herself does half the work of Man.
> Seas, rivers, mountains, forests, deserts, rocks,
> The promontory's height, the depth profound
> Of subterranean, excavated grots,
> Black brow'd, and vaulted high, and yawning wide
> From Nature's structure, or the scoop of Time. (IX, ll. 907-12)

In this poem, according to David B. Morris, Young "explored most ingeniously" "the devotional possibilities of sublimity."[23]

Kirke White undertook to reshape it to his own taste and style in his poem "Time" (p. 17). This is the longest sustained work, though unfinished, that White produced. Little about it is original, but it deserves attention because it represents the young poet's longest serious attempt at the epic form in the sublime mode of religious melancholy.

White takes the first, second, and ninth "Nights" from Young's poem and imitates their combined themes of death, time, and eternity. The obligation to Young is very clear, even though Eleanor Sickels claims she sees more of Gray than Young in it.[24] One could divide the 620 lines of "Time" into a prologue and three parts with each of the three parts corresponding to Young's first, second, and ninth "Nights." The prologue, lines 1-89, includes an invocation for the "Genius of musings" to inspire the poet as he begins his celebration of "the mysteries of Time" a subject whose "dim uncertain gulf" he plans to "explore" (ll. 31-32). The poet has been "tutored" by "divine Philosophy" to prepare him for this "solemn minstrelsy" that he hopes will establish his reputation and survive him long after he has died (ll. 50-62); because his days have had to be given over to unpoetic duties, he has leisure to study and write only at night: "But be the day another's;—let it pass! The night's my own!— They cannot steal my night!" (ll. 74-75). And so it is appropriate as the occasion and theme of his great endeavor that Night should "aid [him] now to magnify / The night of ages" (ll. 83-84).

The reference to "the night of ages" marks an appropriate point of transition to the main section of the poem, for it is to be launched by a meditation on the darkness of night as nature's way of preparing mankind for the long darkness of death. This first main section we might call White's night thoughts on death and mutability, made up of lines 89 through 289. It begins with a call to "behold the world [that] rests" and ends with a confession that one cannot "compass the Almighty mind." First we are to note how the many sleepers are listening to "the warning voice / Of Nature": that sleep is like death, though death will be of "far longer span" (ll. 103-106). Time is, then, but a flight of moments rushing into the great darkness of death, something we are supposed to realize when we contemplate the eternity of the past and the eternity of the future.

White subdivides this first main section into a catalog of time past (introduced by an *ubi sunt* refrain, "where are the heroes of ages past?" l. 133) and a picture of time future when another poet like himself will look into the distant past to the very time in which Kirke White lives, and that future poet will ask, "Where now is Britain?" (l. 193) just as White now asks, "Where is Rome?" (l. 177). All has or will fall before the ruin of Time, a dismaying thought that drives the poet to this conclusion, ending the first main section:

> Time past, and Time to come,
> Are always equal; when the world began
> God had existed from eternity. (ll. 279-81)

This conclusion brings the poet close to an insight that he will later celebrate, that God *is* Time (ll. 471-72), but he is not quite ready to grasp its importance, its significant power to free him from the depression into which he has fallen.

He is ready, however, to admit that he cannot comprehend the vast mystery of time as an eternal future and eternal past. He thus begins the second main section with a resigned humility of failure:

> Oh, who can compass the Almighty mind?
> Who can unlock the secrets of the High?
> In speculations of an altitude
> Sublime as this, our reason stands confessed
> Foolish, and insignificant, and mean. (ll. 290-94)

Especially when he asks if "the less [can] contain the greater" (ll. 300-301), implying that it cannot, we realize how far White is at this point from the great Romantic poets like Blake and Wordsworth and how much closer he is to his primary source in Young's *Night Thoughts*. But the poet in him does not concede failure so easily, even if the pastor does. For he is, we must recognize, trying to contain the greater in the less (to use his terms) when he writes his poem.

He goes on in this second main section to contemplate the futility of Philosophy's proud attempts to "unlock the secrets of the High." First he shows, in lines 310 through 344, how "the unlettered hind" and poor "cotter" can behold God and be happy without understanding Him, while the scientist (described in lines 345-71) all too often becomes irreverent or adversary because of his puny wisdom. These thoughts are driving the poet to another startling conclusion: that earthly wisdom only teaches how "earthly things / Are but the transient pageants of an hour" (ll. 371-72). Reality, spiritual reality, is timeless and not comprehensible by reason alone. Then in a long simile White compares life to a sailor who thinks that it is the shoreline that is moving as he passes by it on his ship; what we should realize by now is that "our being 'tis that moves" and "Time moveth not." (ll. 387-94). Therefore, time as mutability is within our mortal selves, while Time as eternity contains us all. White goes on with his sailing metaphor to describe the "weary mariner" who sails into a destructive storm beyond "Cimmerian Bosphorus" (ll. 404-16).

This mariner hopes for better weather when he perceives very trivial signs, such as a slight opening of a cloud or a slight abatement of the wind. The "good man" will look for more fundamental signs that point "far beyond / The sway of tempests" (ll. 417-418). The "only reasonable hope" is for some peace beyond the storm of life, not for some temporary calm within the storm itself. The "proud man" thinks he can control his destiny because he thinks he can either control or outwit the storms of life, but he should look up to the "starry vault" of the heavens and see from the myriad worlds that his is a puny and impotent life of little significance when measured by the things of nature (ll. 439-57). The second main section, having dealt with human illusion and futile learning, concludes with its focus on the trivial value of life that is "bound to the hasty opinions of an hour" (l. 459).

The third, and final, main section is, like Young's ninth "Night," a "consolation" for the sorrows that have accumulated from the meditations so far. Those have been the "complaint" of an anxious poet, and now he seeks a consolation. This imitates poetry in which Marjorie Hope Nicholson has found "the climax of the conception of the 'vast Sublime,'" as she describes the Ninth Night of *Night Thoughts*.[25] White's consolation is possible because he has learned two important truths: that time, as mutability, is an illusion, and that human reason can deal only with time as illusion, not time as reality. This second truth is essentially a lesson in humility, and that lesson prepares one to understand better the nature of Time as reality; with "awe" and "trembling," the poet now sings "a hymn of laud, a solemn canticle" to God:

> of Thee,
> Great beyond comprehension, who Thyself
> Art Time and Space, sublime Infinitude,
> Of Thee has been my song! (ll. 470-73)

"The idea of God as somehow identified with space had an irresistible appeal to an age that was creating the mechanist philosophy," as Ernest Tuveson has observed.[26] And here we have White saying that not only Space but also Time is God. More accurately, Time as *reality* is God, a theme and insight possible only to one who has meditated on time as illusion. The "consolation" is possible now because the poet will "leave [his] vain laments" and sing the mercy of God.

That mercy is, as William Blake often asserted in his prophetic poetry, the mercy of Eternity, which uses time to rescue man from time. In psychological terms, awareness of time as a succession of moments will keep consciousness alert until it can be rescued from time-as-flowing to time-as-ecstasy, the unselfconscious experience of joyful satisfaction. In the Christian terms that White was employing to understand the importance of "Time," time as the illusion of succeeding moments came into being at the Fall from grace, but it became the mercy of God's love when it became the vehicle for his great Sacrifice in the Incarnation, and the Crucifixion, and it would be itself destroyed by the Resurrection. The last section of the poem, from line 460 to the end, is White's "halleluiah" for the Resurrection as a promise of spiritual freedom for all men, a freedom from the bondage of time:

> The King! the Comforter! the Christ! He comes
> To burst the bonds of Death, and overturn
> The power of Time! (ll. 584-86)

The last section is a celebration of the Second Coming as a Day of Judgment when "Time shall be no more" and all righteous souls will join in a sublime song of praise (ll. 603-606).

White's poem begins with an image of "the harp of Desolation" swept by the hand of time, suggesting that his own poem will imitate this same "music" of desolation. And so it does as it surveys the wrecks of time, the passage of all things into the vast backward abyss of time: this is the desolation of mutability, servant of death and destruction. The reason of man is confined to the trivial dimension of the moment and doomed to the terrors of annihilation. This "endless mutation" leads to a "dismaying sense / Of human impotence" (ll. 235, 252-53). The "harp of Desolation" is making music of despair midway through its performance. It begins to change its tune in a low key of humility, meditations on humble life, and resignation of intellectual claims. A new music begins to be heard when the poet sings of "the good man's hope" that lies "far beyond" "mortal desolation" (ll. 417, 419). Man cannot "contend with Time— unvanquished Time, / The conqueror of conquerors, and lord / Of desolation" (ll. 559-60). There is a new assurance in the tone now, despite the admission of impotence. For against the adversary, time, there is a stronger hero who will "crush the conqueror of conquerors, / And desolate stern Desolation's lord." That, of course, is the God incarnate, who assumed the bonds of time and broke them asunder.

In some of his details, such as his note that he must devote his days to unpoetic labors, White has some distinctive turns in his rendering of Young's *Night Thoughts*. And in his focus on the single topic of time, he has reduced Young's poem from its intimidating bulk to a manageable expression of a sublime experience. The sublime was inevitable for White, not only because it was an appropriate mode for the epic endeavor that any serious poet must attempt, but also because White's religious and intellectual training were coming together with his poetic calling; he was among those who, as David Morris puts the matter, "agree that sublimity is the touchstone of great poetry," and who also "agree that religious ideas are inherently the most sublime."[27] But White was impatient with the passage of time, complaining that his circumstances did not permit greater freedom for study and contemplation, and so it was only natural for him to try to understand the character of his bondage, as "time." And also it was only natural for him to find in the Christian doctrines of Incarnation and Redemption the keys to his liberation. His own daily sacrifice, as he conceived his life to be, was an enactment of the great Sacrifice of Christ, and

In the Tradition of the Sublime: Poetry for the Mind

Christ's atonement was White's promise of spiritual freedom.

Well could Blake have understood the direction of White's young poetry, for Blake understood how Christ could be a hero of the imagination, even the Imagination itself; he once wrote, commenting on his design for "A Vision of the Last Judgment," that "all things are comprehended in their Eternal Forms in the Divine body of the Saviour the True Vine of Eternity the Human Imagination."[28] Besides their common interest in Jesus as the liberating Imagination, White and Blake shared an interest in rewriting Edward Young's *Night Thoughts*, which Blake rewrote as *The Four Zoas* and White as "Time," a much more modest endeavor, to say the least.

Besides imitating *Night Thoughts* in subject matter, situation, and thematic structure, White's poem adopts its epigrammatic style. For example, Young's verse, often irritatingly end-stopped, bumps along from well-turned phrase to well-turned phrase:

> The bell strikes one. We take no note of time
> But from its loss. To give it then a tongue
> Is wise in man. As if an angel spoke,
> I feel the solemn sound. . . .
> . . . . My hopes and fears
> Start up alarmed, and o'er life's narrow verge
> Look down—on what? a fathomless abyss,
> A dread eternity, how surely mine! (I, 55-58, 62-65)

White, on a comparable theme:

> Chained to the grovelling frailties of the flesh,
> Mere mortal man, unpurged from earthly dross,
> Cannot survey, with fixed and steady eye,
> The dim uncertain gulf, which now the muse,
> Adventurous, would explore; but dizzy grown,
> He topples down the abyss. (p. 18; ll. 28-33)

Young turns the nice phrase:

> Procrastination is the thief of time;
> Year after year it steals, till all are fled. (I, 394-95)
> Youth is not rich in time; it may be, poor. (II, 48)
> Time wasted is existence, used is life. (II, 150)

And so does White:

> But be the day another's;—let it pass!
> The night's my own!—They cannot steal my night! (p. 19; ll. 74-75)

White strives for the same exclamatory tone of Young's poem. The frequent use of exclamations in both poems contributes to the same unpleasant effect produced by the frequent pauses for hemistich verse structure. It is as though both poets want to emphasize how important it is to make every word, every "use" of time and space, seem significant. "We are moving," as Martin Price explains the process of Young's poetry, "from image to figure, from the picture to the dislocation of words that indicates the inadequacy of any picture."[29] Finally, notice how unabashedly White borrows phrases and images. When Young writes how

> Each Moment has its sickle, emulous
> Of Time's enormous scythe, whose ample sweep
> Strikes empires from the root. . . . (I, 193-95)

White echoes with this:

> —not a moment flies
> But puts its sickle in the fields of life,
> And mows it thousands, with their joys and cares. (p. 21; ll. 118-20)

Young reaches for the precise word to tell how the deeps of time yield up nothing of all the drowned hours: "In that great deep, which nothing disembogues" (II, 370); White, missing no touch of the master, explains that on the Day of Judgment all will be revealed: "The bellowing floods shall disembogue their charge" (p. 33; l. 527).

White's use of Young's poem is brazen and bold, but he still manages to make it a thing of his own. This was to be White's main way of learning his art, for he had not much time in his life to strike off in new directions. The final poem we will examine is, again, a bold imitation, but it promises something more original than "Time."

In his ambitious *Christiad* (p. 51) White launched an epic in imitation of Spenser's *Faerie Queene* as the form to contain a narrative structure like Milton's *Paradise Lost,* but it describes a

In the Tradition of the Sublime: Poetry for the Mind 153

situation that developed after Milton's *Paradise Regained* on a theme that White must have thought Spenser and Milton ignored: "To paint the agonies that Jesus bore!" (p. 52; IV, 2), the Passion and Crucifixion of Christ. If Kirke White was nothing else, he was courageous.

Nor should we deny to White our respect for his unerring good taste in this matter, even though we might wonder about his judgment. He did know the best models to imitate, and he did know what needed to be done to satisfy his daemonic insistence upon the religious sublime. White's fantastic virtuosity, ranging through the great works of the English classics, is a remarkable anticipation of similar experiments by Keats and Shelley, not to mention its echo of earlier ones by Coleridge and Southey. White was on a boundary of style and taste, as well as time, dividing the era of Collins, the Wartons, and Young from the era of Blake, Wordsworth, Southey, and Coleridge; in addition, he lived between the two generations of the great Romantics as well, writing after the publication of *The Lyrical Ballads* but well before even the fame of Byron. Given what we have of his poetry, and seeing how it reflects many styles and traditions, White was poised to fall backwards or leap forward just when he died.

His great hero was inevitably the Christ of the Passion, for in the sufferings and death of Jesus the poet could too easily see himself, as would Shelley soon afterwards. It seems right, then, to conclude this study of Kirke White with a comment on his *Christiad*, for it identifies him as an heir of contradictory values, styles, and themes. He knew by instinct, if not by experience, that if he were to survive as a genuine poet, he must find a way to unify, or at least sort out, these contradictions in himself and in his heritage. Between reason and imagination he sought for a union in religious faith; between the descriptive picturesque and the lyrical music of beauty he attempted the intellectual sublime; and between his personal melancholy and Christian optimism he reached for a resolution through Milton's myth and Spenser's allegory. Thus *The Christiad* seemed to White a new, if not a last, chance to "reanimate" his "lay" (p. 65; Book II, stanza 2).

The poem was left unfinished (like so many works by the great Romantics) at White's death. As we have it, there are two books, one almost complete with thirty-two and one-half Spenserian stanzas, and the other barely begun, with two stanzas (which suggest that they were composed long after the stanzas of the first book). The first book can be divided into four parts for description and commentary. The first part includes stanzas 1 through 5, and it constitutes the prologue of invocation by the poet. He addresses two powers to help him "sing the Cross": the the "white-robed angel choirs" and Urania, the heavenly muse of astronomy. He asks the angel choirs to "awake [his] slumbering spirit from its dream" of life (I, i, 8) and to teach [him] how to exalt the high mysterious theme" (I, i, 9). He immediately begins to describe a scene of urban desolation; in stanzas 2 and 3, he mourns the destruction of Salem (i.e., Jerusalem), "aghast" at what he envisions, like a "pilgrim" made "mute" by the great waste of the "void profound." What has caused this scene of ruin over which "stern Destruction laughs"? That great city had persecuted and then destroyed the Son of God, and she in turn has been destroyed. The story of how this occurred is to be the subject of White's epic poem. The scene of desolation, representative of all fallen civilzation, leads the poet to contemplate the desolation and suffering of the Man whose death has caused Salem's fall into ruin.

But he needs more divine assistance to be able "to paint the agonies that Jesus bore." He calls upon Urania, that same muse invoked by Milton in *Paradise Lost,* Books I and VII, to assist him in his epic work. Urania, in the company of "mild crusaders," is called by White to "give him eloquence," to throw over him a "solemn stole" that will "clothe him for the fight with energy divine" (I, v, 1-9). The prologue is, then, an elaborately conceived invocation for help to describe two main scenes: vast desolation in the city of Salem, and the profound personal agonies of Jesus. These scenes typify themes common to Kirke White's poetry, as we have seen, and the prologue to *The Christiad* is, even with its conventional form of invocation, the most authentic section of the first book, because it communicates the poet's compelling sense of desolation and suffering common to himself and all mankind.

The second part, stanzas vi-xi, begins at the point where Milton's *Paradise Regained* concluded with its narrative of Satan's temptation of Christ:

> When from the temple's lofty summit prone,
>   Satan, o'ercome, fell down; and throned there,

In the Tradition of the Sublime: Poetry for the Mind 155

> The son of God confessed, in splendour shone:
> Swift as the glancing sunbeam cuts the air,
> Mad with defeat, and yelling his despair. (p. 53; stanza vi)

This echoes Milton's lines describing how Satan failed to tempt Christ into defying death by leaping from the holy Temple of Jersusalem:[30]

> To whom thus Jesus. Also it is written,
> Tempt not the Lord thy God; he said and stood.
> But Satan smitten with amazement fell. . . .
> . . . . .
> So after many a foil the Tempter proud,
> Renewing fresh assaults, amidst his pride
> Fell whence he stood to see his Victor fall. (IV, 560-62, 569-71)

White is inspired by this, the third, fall of Satan, and he proceeds to describe in stanzas vii-xi the sublime and terrifying event, as Satan and all his crew retreat to the frozen regions of the North Pole, thus beginning the third part. That region with its vast nothingness and frozen waste was a popular subject of epic poetry from at least as early as James Thomson, and it is even possible that White knew the poetry in which Dante placed Satan in a frozen region at the center of the earth.

After he has brought Satan to his new kingdom in the North White proceeds to describe the fallen angels in terms much like the ones Milton used to describe them at the beginning of *Paradise Lost,* especially Satan's summoning of followers to a great council of war. This council takes up the remainder of the first book. It begins with a description of Satan, passionately defiant even after still another defeat:

> Fixed as Fate
> I am His foe! —Yea, though His pride should design
> To soothe mine ire with half His regal state,
> Still would I burn with fixed unalterable hate. (p. 56; stanza xiv)

White is as fascinated by the passion of Satan as he says he is by the passion of Christ. "As he says he is," because White does not actually get to the point in his poem where he deals with the real, or announced, subject of the epic: "the agonies that Jesus bore." Like the Romantic poets, White seems captivated by the great Adversary; even when he rewrites the "epic" of Christ's victory narrated in *Paradise Regained,* our poet tells the story from Satan's point of view.

That story, reduced to two episodes of temptation, is the subject of Satan's first speech to his fallen kingdom. In stanzas xv-xxii, Satan tells what has happened to him since he last left them to tempt Jesus into a betrayal of his holy mission. Echoing *Paradise Regained,* Book I, White has Satan explain how he accosted Jesus in the desert, pretending to be an old man tempting Jesus to satisfy his hunger by turning stones to bread (in this episode White may have realized that behind Milton's rendition was Spenser's tale of Archimago and the Redcrosse Knight, although he may not have known about Giles Fletcher's similar handling of the event in his poem of *Christ's Victorie and Triumph,* 1610, that also lay behind Milton's story).

After the last temptation atop Jerusalem's Temple, Satan fell again back to this present predicament: "Senseless and stunned I lay; till casting round / My half unconscious gaze, I saw the Foe [Jesus] / Borne on a car of roses to the ground, / By volant angels" (p. 59; stanza xxii). White modifies Milton's "floating couch" with this "car of roses," which may seem merely quaint or a delicate touch by a poet of sensibility. But long before Kirke White, Dante used the rose for his vision of paradise, and not long after White's death Goethe would use roses to shower a blessing on Faust and as a punishment of Mephistopheles, while Faust's immortal essence is wafted aloft by a chorus of angels. But White's attention continues to be focused on Satan, still recovering from his latest defeat. He repeats his defiance of God in a speech that ends the third part of Book I, enthralled by a vision of Jesus's suffering and death, which he vows to bring about: " 'I hear His cries! / He faints—He falls—and lo!—'tis true, ye powers, He dies' " (p. 60; stanza xxiv).

The fourth, and final, part of Book I is a description of the other devils' response to their chief's speech. We are invited to view Satan as his followers see him, uplifted by his vow of continuing defiance and excited by his vision of Christ's suffering:

> with his foot advanced
> And chest inflated, motionless he stood,
>   While under his uplifted shield he glanced,
>   With straining eyeball fixed, like one entranced,
> On viewless air. (p. 60; stanza xxv)

This is the theatrical pose of a hero, though a braggart warrior victimized by his own passionate fancy, and still fascinating to Kirke White, nevertheless. He shows us the power of Christ's suffering by the effect it has on Christ's great enemy (an ancient device of poets, from the time when Homer suggested the beauty of Helen by the effect it had on the old men of Troy).

The remainder of this part is taken up by a speech of Moloch, who scoffs at Satan for his failure: " 'This comes of distant counsels! Here behold / The fruits of cunning!' " (p. 61; stanza xxviii). Satan responds with an apologia, in prose: " 'Ye powers of Hell, I am no coward. I proved this of old. . . . True bravery is as remote from rashness as from hesitation' " (pp. 62-63). These are sentiments with which White could surely agree, but they come unfortunately from the enemy, the cause of his hero's passion and death. White may have intended to leave Satan's speech in prose, thus signaling its lack of divine truth, or abuse of truth, through its lack of poetic form; or the poet was not yet able to make poetry out of the speech, a poetry that might need to be ironic or satiric of matters that White valued in themselves, though not in the employ of evil. After Satan's final speech, the God of Fire, "Mecashpim," rises to begin the era of desolation, wandering over the earth "searching for the flame it loves" (p. 63). At this point, if not earlier in the prose passage of Satan's speech, the poem begins to fall apart; the last two stanzas concern the desolation and destruction about to be launched by Satan's forces.

What was to become Book II opens with two stanzas of personal exhaustion and hope for renewal of spirit to complete the poem before the poet dies. So far the task has been "self-rewarding," a satisfying attempt to write of deeds "far loftier than beseem / The lyre which I in early days have strung." But the effort has been exhausting ("now my spirits faint"), and he needs help to "reanimate the lay." Only God can help him, for his fear is that he will not be able to complete his gift of poetry before Death cuts short his life's journey:

I am a youthful traveller in the way,
And this slight boon would consecrate to Thee,
Ere I with Death shake hands, and smile that I am free. (p. 65)

The metaphor of shaking hands is bathetic, but the final words of this epic effort are words appropriate for concluding an examination of White's poetry, cut off as it was before he could find himself in the mature company of the great Romantic poets whose figures loom so large in the era of his short life.

Notes and References

Preface

1. "An Account of the Life of Henry Kirke White," *The Complete Works of Henry Kirke White* (Boston: N. H. Whitaker, 1831), p. 3. First published in London in 1807. References hereafter will be to *Complete Works*.
2. The quotation is taken from *Don Juan and Other Satirical Poems*, ed. Louis I. Bredvold (New York: The Odyssey Press, 1935), pp. 33–34.
3. Letter to Dallas, 21 August 1811. *Bryon's Letters and Journals*, Vol. 2: 1810–1812, *"Famous in My time,"* ed. Leslie A. Marchand (Cambridge, Mass.: Harvard University Press, 1973), p. 76.
4. Letter to Dallas, 27 August 1811. Ibid., p. 82.

Chapter One

1. Letter to Neville, September 1799. *The Life and Remains* (London: J. F. Dove, 1827), p. 208.
2. Letter to Neville, 26 June 1800. Ibid., p. 209.
3. Ibid., p. 210
4. Ibid., p. 211.
5. Southey's "Account of the Life," *Complete Works*, p. 10.
6. Letter to Mr. Booth, 12 August 1801. *Life and Remains*, p. 221.
7. Ibid., p. 222.
8. Southey's "Account of the Life," p. 14.
9. Ibid., p. 19.
10. Ibid., p. 20.
11. Letter to Neville, 1803. *Life and Remains*, p. 230.
12. He wrote Neville that their "father made some heavy complaints when I was at home; and though I am induced to believe that he is enough harassed to render it very excusable, yet I cannot but feel strongly the peculiarity of my situation; and, at my age, feel ashamed that I should add to his burdens." 20 August 1805. Ibid., pp. 302–303.
13. He wrote Maddock, describing the episode and the doctor's opinion that "it looks towards epilepsy." July 1806. Ibid., p. 352.
14. Southey's "Account of the Life," pp. 22–23.
15. *History of English Thought in the Eighteenth Century*. Vol. 1,

Chapter 3, Harbinger Books Edition (New York: Harcourt, 1962), pp. 76-156.

16. Ibid., pp. 157-234.
17. *Analogy of Religion*, 3rd. ed. (Philadelphia: J. B. Lippincott & Co., 1860), pp. 310, 126.
18. Letter to Maddock, 31 January 1805, *Life and Remains*, p. 277.
19. "Melancholy Hours (No. III)." Ibid., p. 403.
20. *Natural Theology* (Boston, Mass.: Gould, Kendall and Lincoln, 1837), p. 26.
21. "Reflections," *Complete Works*, p. 419 (White's italics).
22. "Melancholy Hours (No. IX)," *Life and Remains*, p. 440.
23. Letter to Mr. Serjeant Rough, 17 February 1805. Ibid., pp. 282, 284.
24. Letter to Neville, 25 June 1800. Ibid., pp. 212-13 (White's italics).
25. Ibid., p. 213.
26. "Melancholy Hours (No. IX)." Ibid., pp. 432-33.
27. "Melancholy Hours (No. III)." Ibid., pp. 402-403.
28. Letter to B. Maddock [undated]. Ibid., pp. 234, 235.
29. Letter to Mr. R. A. ——, 18 April 1804. Ibid., p. 236.
30. Letter to Neville [undated]. Ibid., pp. 240-41.
31. Letter to B. Maddock, 7 July 1804. Ibid., pp. 256-57.
32. Letter to Mr. Serjeant Rough, 24 July 1804. Ibid., pp. 259-60.
33. Letter "To The Editor," 9 July 1804. Ibid., p. 259.
34. Letter to Mr. Serjeant Rough, 17 February 1805. Ibid., p. 283.
35. Letter to B. Maddock, September 1804. Ibid., p. 263.
36. Letter to Neville, 19 December 1805. Ibid., p. 324.
37. Letter to B. Maddock, 17 February 1806. Ibid., p. 333 (White's italics).
38. Letter to Mr. R. W. A., 18 August 1806. Ibid., pp. 363-64 (White's italics).
39. Letter to B. Maddock, 22 September 1806. Ibid., p. 366.
40. Letter to Neville, 11 April 1801. Ibid., pp. 216-17.
41. Letter to Neville, April 1801. Ibid., p. 220.
42. "Melancholy Hours (No. V)." Ibid., p. 414.
43. "Melancholy Hours (No. III)." Ibid., p. 403.
44. "Remarks on the English Poets: Sternhold and Hopkins," Ibid., p. 379.
45. "Remarks on the English Poets: Warton," Ibid., pp. 381-383.
46. "Melancholy Hours (No. I)." Ibid., p. 392.
47. "Melancholy Hours (No. III)." Ibid., p. 403.
48. "Melancholy Hours (No. XII)." Ibid., p. 449.
49. "Melancholy Hours (No. VII)." Ibid., p. 422.
50. Letter "(Supposed to be Addressed) To Mrs. West" [undated].Ibid., p. 340.
51. Letter to Mr. P. Thompson, 8 April 1806. Ibid., p. 344.

Notes and References

Chapter Two

1. Letter to Neville, 26 June 1800. *The Life and Remains*, p. 210.
2. Letter to Neville, April 1801. Ibid., p. 219; to Neville, April 1805, p. 286; refers to the *Spectator* in a letter to Mr. ?, 15 August 1806, p. 358; "Melancholy Hours (No. II)," p. 396.
3. *The Rambler*, ed. W. J. Bate and Albrecht B. Strauss. 3 vols. The Yale Edition (New Haven, Conn.: Yale University Press, 1969), I, 95.
4. *The Citizen of the World*, ed. Arthur Friedman, Vol. 2 of *Collected Works of Oliver Goldsmith* (Oxford: At the Clarendon Press, 1966), p. 276.
5. *Life of Johnson.* Oxford Standard Authors edition (London: Oxford University Press, 1960), pp. 825, 856.
6. Quotations from the texts of *Melancholy Hours* are taken from *The Life and Remains of Henry Kirke White of Nottingham: Late of St. John's College, Cambridge* (London: J. F. Dover, 1827). Page numbers for quotations will appear in parentheses in the text of my discussion.
7. Eleanor M. Sickels, *The Gloomy Egoist: Moods and Themes of Melancholy from Gray to Keats* (New York: Columbia University Press, 1932), p. 253.
8. Ernst Cassirer, *The Philosophy of the Enlightenment*, trans. Fritz C. A. Koelln and James P. Pettegrove (1951; rpt. Boston: Beacon Press, 1955). p. 153.
9. Sister M. Kevin Whelan, S.S.J., *Enthusiasm in English Poetry of the Eighteenth Century (1700-1744)* Folcroft, Pa.: Folcroft Press, Inc., 1970), p. 75.
10. Margery Bailey, "Edward Young," in *The Age of Johnson: Essays Presented to Chauncey Brewster Tinker*, ed. Frederick W. Hilles (New Haven and London: Yale University Press, 1949), p. 198.
11. David B. Morris, *The Religious Sublime: Christian Poetry and Critical Tradition in 18th-Century England* (Lexington, Ky.: University Press of Kentucky, 1972), p. 152.

Chapter Three

1. *The Poetical Works of Akenside and Beattie* (Boston: Houghton Mifflin and Co., n.d.). Page numbers in the text are to this volume.
2. Joseph Addison's essays on "The Pleasures of the Imagination" appeared in the *Spectator*, Nos. 411-21; Shaftesbury's *Characteristics of Men, Manners, Opinions, Times* was published in 1711; Edmund Burke's *Philosophical Enquiry into the Origin of Our Ideas of the Sublime and the Beautiful* in 1757 (or, as some think, 1756), and David Hume's essay "Of the Standard of Taste" in 1757. Richard Payne Knight's *Analytical Inquiry into the Principles of Taste* was already in its second edition (1805) shortly before Kirke White's death.
3. William Gilpin's *Essays on Picturesque Beauty* appeared in 1792,

and Uvedale Price's *Essay on the Picturesque* in 1794. The quotation is from Uvedale Price, cited by Martin Price, *To the Palace of Wisdom: Studies in Order and Energy from Dryden to Blake* (Garden City, N.Y.: Doubleday, 1964), p. 381.

4. Sickels, p. 47.

5. All quotations from White's poetry are taken from *The Poetical Works of Henry Kirke White*. The Aldine Edition of the British Poets (London: Bell and Daldy, 1867). I have chosen this edition because it conveniently arranges White's poetry into types that roughly coincide with my own arrangement for purposes of discussion. Line numbers are supplied by me.

6. Robert Arnold Aubin, *Topographical Poetry in XVIII-England* (1936; rpt. New York: Kraus Reprint Corp., 1966), pp. 144-45.

7. P. W. K. Stone, *The Art of Poetry, 1750-1820* (London: Routledge and Kegan Paul Ltd., 1967), p. 83.

8. Walter John Hipple, Jr., *The Beautiful, the Sublime, and the Picturesque in Eighteenth-Century British Aesthetic Theory* (Carbondale: Southern Illinois University Press, 1957), p. 186.

9. Patricia Meyer Spacks, *The Poetry of Vision: Five Eighteenth-Century Poets* (Cambridge, Mass.: Harvard University Press, 1967), p. 2.

10. John Dixon Hunt, *The Figure in the Landscape: Poetry, Painting, and Gardening during the Eighteenth Century* (Baltimore and London: The Johns Hopkins University Press, 1976), p. 157.

11. Hipple, p. 210.

12. Sickels, p. 253.

13. Thus has C. Day Lewis translated Aeneas's phrase, "sunt lacrimae rerum," in Book I of *The Aeneid*, Doubleday Anchor Book (New York: Doubleday, 1953), p. 26.

14. Ralph M. Williams, "Thomson and Dyer: Poet and Painter," in *The Age of Johnson*, p. 209.

15. J. R. Watson, *Picturesque Landscape and English Romantic Poetry* (London: Hutchinson Educational Ltd., 1970), p. 19.

16. Spacks, p. 47.

17. Earl R. Wasserman, "The Inherent Values of Eighteenth-Century Personification," *PMLA* 65 (1950): 460.

18. Lawrence Lipking, *The Ordering of the Arts in Eighteenth-Century England* (Princeton, N.J.: Princeton University Press, 1970), p. 381.

19. See, for example, the Catalogue of Fuseli's works in *Henry Fuseli: 1741-1825*, published by the Trustees of the Tate Gallery (London, 1975), pp. 51-138.

20. C. V. Deane, *Aspects of Eighteenth Century Nature Poetry* (1935; rpt. London: Frank Cass and Company, Ltd., 1967), p. 75.

21. Wasserman, p. 446.

22. Spacks, p. 194.

23. "To the eighteenth-century reader . . . epithets served as aids to visualization." Chester F. Chapin, *Personification in Eighteenth-Century English Poetry* (New York: King's Crown Press, Columbia University, 1955), p. 63.

24. Bertrand Harris Bronson, "Personification Reconsidered," in *Facets of the Enlightenment: Studies in English Literature and Its Context*, by Bertrand Harris Bronson (Berkeley and Los Angeles: University of California Press, 1968), pp. 146, 147.

Chapter Four

1. Quotations from Collins's poems are taken from *The Poems of Gray, Collins and Goldsmith*, ed. Roger Lonsdale. Longman's Annotated English Poets (London: Longman Group Limited, 1969), pp. 355–66.

2. Besides echoes of Collins we may hear in White's poems themselves, including the explicit borrowing from "The Passions" acknowledged in a note to "Gondoline," *Poetical Works*, p. 194, we have White's letter to his brother, in which he offers to let Neville read Johnson's *Lives of the Poets* that White had lately purchased; dated from Nottingham, April 1801, *Complete Works*, p. 223. We may assume, then, the "Life of Collins" was read by Kirke White, for he shows many signs of being a voracious reader.

3. "Toward Literary History," in *Beyond Formalism: Literary Essays 1958-1970*, by Geoffrey H. Hartman (New Haven: Yale University Press, 1970), p. 372.

4. *The Anxiety of Influence: A Theory of Poetry* (New York: Oxford University Press 1973), pp. 110–11.

5. *The Romantic Sublime: Studies in the Structure and Psychology of Transcendence* (Baltimore and London: The Johns Hopkins University Press, 1976), p. 18; see also the detailed analysis of Collins, pp. 107–35.

6. Wasserman, p. 454.

7. He offers to lend it to Neville in a letter dated from Nottingham, April 1801. *Complete Works*, p. 223.

8. *A Philosophical Enquiry*, ed. J. T. Boulton (London: Routledge and Kegan Paul, 1958), pp. 121, 122. Quotations from Burke's *Enquiry* are taken from this edition, with page numbers in parentheses hereafter.

9. Letter to Mr. Serjeant Rough, 17 February 1805, and letter to Capel Lofft, 10 September 1805. *Complete Works*, pp. 273, 290–91.

10. Patricia Meyer Spacks, *The Insistence of Horror: Aspects of the Supernatural in Eighteenth-Century Poetry* (Cambridge, Mass.: Harvard University Press, 1962), p. 89.

11. "From Action to Image: Theories of the Lyric in the Eighteenth Century," in *Critics and Criticism*, ed. R. S. Crane (Chicago: University of Chicago Press, 1952), p. 455.
12. Ibid., pp. 428-29.
13. Letter to Neville, dated from Nottingham, 26 June 1800. *Complete Works*, p. 215.
14. Maclean, p. 415.
15. *Philosophy in a New Key: A Study in the Symbolism of Reason, Rite, and Art*, 2nd ed., A Mentor Book (New York: New American Library, 1951), p. 204.
16. Letter to Mrs. West, no date specified, but placed so as to suggest April 1806. *Complete Works*, p. 320.
17. Weiskel, p. 6.
18. "The Pre-Romantic or Post-Augustan Mode," in *Facets of the Enlightenment*, p. 171.

Chapter Five

1. Thomas Weiskel has explained the importance of Locke for any study of the sublime as a matter of crisis, for "the Lockean model subverts the autonomy of the mind or soul; the mind is not its own place, but the space in which semiotic sublimations occur. It cannot control the making of meaning, though increasingly the imagination is granted a limited autonomy, a license to compose the ideas in novel combinations." *The Romantic Sublime*, pp. 17-18.
2. Hipple, pp. 96-97.
3. Letter to Neville, dated from Nottingham, 11 April 1801. *Complete Works*, p. 220.
4. "Everyone after Burke either imitates him or borrows from him or feels it is necessary to refute him." Hipple, p. 83.
5. *Ruins and Empire: The Evolution of a Theme in Augustan and Romantic Literature* (Pittsburgh: University of Pittsburgh Press, 1977), p. 77.
6. Quotations from "Winter" are taken from *The Complete Poetical Works of James Thomson*, ed. J. Logie Robertson (1908; rpt. London: Oxford University Press, 1951), pp. 185-238.
7. Sickels, p. 254.
8. Goldstein, p. 82.
9. Eleanor Sickels sees little of Gray in the poem either. She thinks "the idea is more after Goldsmith's lines about the hope of returning home to die," p. 101.
10. Quotations from Parnell's poem are taken from *The Poetical Works of Thomas Parnell*, ed. George A. Aitken (London: George Bell and Sons, 1894), pp. 93-96.
11. Quotations from Blair's poem are taken from *The Works of the*

English Poets, From Chaucer to Cowper, ed. Alexander Chalmers (1810; rpt. New York: Greenwood Press, 1969), XV, 63-68; the "sottish sexton" passage is on p. 66.

12. The quotation from Hervey's *Meditations among the Tombs* is from *Meditations and Contemplations*, Two Volumes in One (London: C. Cooke, 1798?), p. 16.

13. Quotations from "The Pleasures of Melancholy" are taken from *The Three Wartons: A Choice of Their Verse*, ed. Eric Partridge (London: The Scholartis Press, 1927), pp. 101-12.

14. "The Sublime Poem: Pictures and Powers," *Yale Review* 58: 2 (1968): 199.

15. Ibid., p. 207.

16. *The Rhetoric of Science: A Study of Scientific Ideas and Imagery in Eighteenth-Century English Poetry* (Berkeley and Los Angeles: University of California Press, 1966), p. 205.

17. Weiskel, p. 105.

18. Harold Bloom, *Figures of Capable Imagination* (New York: The Seabury Press, 1976), p. 7.

19. Ibid., p. 8.

20. Quotations from "Religious Musings" are taken from *The Complete Poetical Works of Samuel Taylor Coleridge*, ed. Ernest Hartley Coleridge, 1 (Oxford: At the Clarendon Press, 1912), 108-25.

21. *The Prelude, or Growth of a Poet's Mind*, ed. Ernest De Selincourt. 2nd ed. rev. Helen Darbishire (Oxford: At the Clarendon Press, 1959), Book VI, ll. 532, 538-39 (p. 208; the 1805-1806 version); ll. 599, 604-605 (p. 209; the 1850 version).

22. Quotations from *Night Thoughts* are taken from *Young's Night Thoughts*, with life, critical dissertation, and explanatory notes by George Gilfillan (Edinburgh: James Nichol, 1853).

23. Morris, p. 145.

24. Sickels, p. 146.

25. *Mountain Gloom and Mountain Glory: The Development of the Aesthetics of the Infinite* (Ithaca, N.Y.: Cornell University Press, 1959), p. 362.

26. "Space, Deity, and the 'Natural Sublime,'" *Modern Language Quarterly* 12: 1 (1951): 27.

27. Morris, p. 169.

28. *The Poetry and Prose of William Blake*, ed. David V. Erdman (Garden City, N.Y.: Doubleday, 1970), p. 545.

29. Martin Price, p. 208.

30. Quotations from *Paradise Regained* are taken from *John Milton: The Complete Poems and Major Prose*, ed. Merritt Y. Hughes (New York: The Odyssey Press, 1957), p. 528.

Selected Bibliography

PRIMARY SOURCES

Melancholy Hours, and other essays originally published in 1801 by *Monthly Preceptor, Monthly Visitor,* and *Monthly Mirror,* were published together in *The Life and Remains,* for which Southey prepared his "Account of the Life," in 1807.
Clifton Grove, a Sketch in Verse, with Other Poems. London: Vernon and Hood, 1803.

(A great many editions of Kirke White's writings were published during the century following his death: the ones consulted for this study are given below.)

The Life and Remains of Henry Kirke White, of Nottingham: Late of St. John's College, Cambridge. London: J. F. Dove, 1827.
The Complete Works of Henry Kirke White. With an account of his life by Robert Southey. Boston: N. H. Whitaker, 1831.
The Poetical Works of Henry Kirke White and James Grahame. Edinburgh: James Nichol, 1856.
The Poetical Works of Henry Kirke White; also containing his Melancholy Hours. With a Memoir by Robert Southey. Boston: Crosby, Nichols, Lee & Company, 1860.
The Poetical Works of Henry Kirke White. The Aldine Edition of The British Poets. London: Bell and Daldy, 1867.

SECONDARY SOURCES

AUBIN, ROBERT ARNOLD. *Topographical Poetry in XVIII-England.* 1936; rpt. New York: Kraus Reprint Corporation, 1966, pp. 144–45. Contains one of the few modern commentaries on Kirke White's poetry. Looks at "Clifton Grove" as an example of topographical poetry in the period.
BLUNDEN, EDMUND. "Thoughts on Kirke White." *Renaissance and Modern Studies* 6(1962), 147–151. Calls for the recovery of any papers by Kirke White which have not been made public or published. Argues that there is a need to establish a more reliable text, since

Southey was probably unable to produce the best text possible for White's poetry. Suggests that we should think of Shelley and Keats as followers of White.

BRONSON, BERTRAND HARRIS. "The Pre-Romantic or Post-Augustan Mode." *Journal of English Literary History* 20: 1 (1953); rpt. *Facets of the Enlightenment*, by Bertrand Bronson. Berkeley and Los Angeles: University of California Press, 1968, pp. 159-72. Describes the era as one of "eclectic habits" and "uncommittedness."

———. "Personification Reconsidered." *New Light on Dr. Johnson*. Ed. F. W. Willis. New Haven: Yale University Press, 1959; rpt. *Facets of the Enlightenment*, pp. 119-52. Explains that eighteenth-century poets needed to use personification as a means of keeping private concerns in the background while raising their interests to the level of generalization.

BURKE, EDMUND. *A Philosophical Enquiry into the Origin of Our Ideas of the Sublime and Beautiful*. Ed. J. T. Boulton. London: Routledge and Kegan Paul, 1958. First published in 1757 (?), this is a landmark essay on the distinction between two key terms of aesthetics in the century. Burke argues that terror is the chief characteristic of the sublime experience.

BYRON, LORD. "English Bards and Scotch Reviewers: A Satire." *Don Juan and Other Satirical Poems*. Ed. Louis I. Bredvold. New York: The Odyssey Press, 1935, pp. 3-43. Lines 831-48, pp. 33-34, constitute one of the earliest expressions of appreciation for White's poetry.

———. Letters to Robert Charles Dallas, dated August 21, 1811, and August 27, 1811. *Bryon's Letters and Journals*. Vol. 2: 1810-1812, *"Famous in My Time."* Ed. Leslie A. Marchand. Cambridge, Mass.: The Belknap Press of Harvard University Press, 1973, pp. 75-77, 81-83. These letters maintain the genius and good taste of White against the differing opinion of Dallas.

GAY, PETER. *The Enlightenment: An Interpretation*. Vol. 1. *The Rise of Modern Paganism*. New York: Alfred A. Knopf, 1967. Vol. 2. *The Science of Freedom*. New York: Alfred A. Knopf, 1969. Analyzes the rich diversity of ideas generated by the eighteenth-century philosophes of Europe and America.

GILFILLAN, GEORGE. "The Life and Writings of Henry Kirke White." *The Poetical Works of Henry Kirke White and James Grahame*. Edinburgh: James Nichol, 1856, pp. vii-xxii. Praises White's essays as "really superior," deplores the suffering of the young poet, observes that the poetry is "generally measured, and regulated to the brink of tameness," and remarks that Southey's *Remains of Henry Kirke White* is "one of the most pleasing and popular books in British literature."

GOLDSTEIN, LAURENCE. *Ruins and Empire: The Evolution of a Theme in*

Augustan and Romantic Literature. Pittsburgh: University of Pittsburgh Press, 1977. Discusses the phenomenon of eighteenth-century interest in "graveyard literature," maintaining that it is primarily an antipastoral mode of writing.

HIPPLE, WALTER JOHN, JR. *The Beautiful, the Sublime, and the Picturesque in Eighteenth-Century British Aesthetic Theory.* Carbondale: Southern Illinois University Press, 1957. An important survey and analysis of the major British philosophers of aesthetics; makes an especially vigorous defense of Burke's *Enquiry* as a "brilliant if incomplete system, of merit not historical but absolute and permanent."

MACLEAN, NORMAN. "From Action to Image: Theories of the Lyric in the Eighteenth-Century." *Critics and Criticism.* Ed. R. S. Crane. Chicago: University of Chicago Press, 1952, pp. 408-60. A major contribution to the history of literature in eighteenth-century England; shows how the development and practice of the ode coincided with and reenforced developing discussions of the beautiful and the sublime.

MORRIS, DAVID B. *The Religious Sublime: Christian Poetry and Critical Tradition in 18th-Century England.* Lexington: University Press of Kentucky, 1972. Examines the important consequences for eighteenth-century British poetry after Dennis stressed Milton's sublimity as a religious poet.

NICHOLSON, MARJORIE HOPE. *Mountain Gloom and Mountain Glory: The Development of the Aesthetics of the Infinite.* Ithaca, N.Y.: Cornell University Press, 1959. Shows how the literature of the century reflects a passage "from Infinite God through vast Nature to the soul of man; from the soul of man through vast Nature back to Infinite God." This is a rich documentation of the ways science and religion were accommodated in eighteenth-century British writing.

PRICE, MARTIN. "The Sublime Poem: Pictures and Powers." *Yale Review* 58:2 (1968): 194-213. This is an important and useful essay for understanding how the experience of the sublime works in poetry; it is described as a dramatic encounter of the self with the self in "a new state of awareness."

SICKELS, ELEANOR M. *The Gloomy Egoist: Moods and Themes of Melancholy from Gray to Keats.* New York: Columbia University Press, 1932. Contains the only serious literary criticism of White's poetry that I know of from this century; besides containing helpful comments on White's poetry, it carefully documents the significant treatments of melancholy in eighteenth-century and Romantic literature.

SOUTHEY, ROBERT. "An Account of the Life of Henry Kirke White." 1807; rpt. Boston: N. H. Whitaker, 1831, pp. 3-44. A very well written essay in appreciation of White's life and writings; establishes the main points for beginning any study of the poet.

SPACKS, PATRICIA MEYER. *The Insistence of Horror: Aspects of the Supernatural in Eighteenth-Century Poetry.* Cambridge, Mass.: Harvard University Press, 1962. Shows how most of the poets who dealt with the supernatural were trying "to find a way of . . . giving the supernatural human validity."

———. *The Poetry of Vision: Five Eighteenth-Century Poets.* Cambridge, Mass.: Harvard University Press, 1967. Analyzes the various uses of visual imagery in the poetry of Thomson, Collins, Gray, Smart, and Cowper; important for making distinctions between "recorded visions of reality" and "visionary" departures from "Actuality."

STEPHEN, LESLIE. *History of English Thought in the Eighteenth Century.* 2 vols. A Harbinger Book. London: Harcourt, Brace & World, 1962. First published in 1876, third edition 1902. Still perhaps the best survey of major ideas and intellectual currents in eighteenth-century Britain. The first volume describes the philosophical basis for the thought of the century, and then it proceeds to outline the major religious trends, including deism and the later theology of Paley and the Unitarians. The second volume concentrates on moral, political, and economic trends of thought, culminating in the rise of Romanticism.

TODD, JOHN. "Introduction" to *The Poetical Works of Henry Kirke White.* Boston: Crosby, Nichols, Lee & Company, 1860, pp. 11-55. An impressionistic essay that praises White for his "genuine Poetry and Evangelical Piety." Very interesting as an example of the continuing popularity of White's writings in America as well as in Britain.

TUVESON, ERNEST. "Space, Deity, and the 'Natural Sublime.'" *Modern Language Quarterly* 12:1 (1951): 20-38. Shows how the experience of the "natural sublime" is an identification of God with space.

WARD, WILLIAMS, S. "Was Henry Kirke White a Victim of The Review Press?" *Modern Language Notes* 60: 5(May 1945), 337-338. Argues that generally the reviews of White's volume of poetry were "mild and restrained," and some were favorable. "Only two of the nineteen known reviews were unfavorable."

WASSERMAN, EARL R. "The Inherent Values of Eighteenth-Century Personification." *Publications of the Modern Language Association of America* 65(1950): 435-63. Explains why the personified abstraction was considered to be "one of the most energetic activities of the imagination" in eighteenth-century poetry; suggests that this figure of speech "was usually associated with the esthetics of the sublime."

WEISKEL, THOMAS. *The Romantic Sublime: Studies in the Structure and Psychology of Transcendence.* Baltimore and London: The Johns Hopkins University Press, 1976. Although obscured by the jargon of psychology and the "Yale critics'" theories of poetic influence, this is an important discussion of its subject, focusing on the "Romantic sublime" as a way of understanding the phenomenon we have come to call "natural supernaturalism." The special thesis is that the "rhetorical sublime" is "structurally cognate" with the "'natural' sublime."

WILLEY, BASIL. *The Eighteenth Century Background: Studies on the Idea of Nature in the Thought of the Period.* Beacon Paperback. Boston: Beacon Press, by arrangement with Columbia University Press, 1961. First published in 1940 by Chatto and Windus, Ltd., London. This book owes much to Leslie Stephen's *History of English Thought,* cited above; however, it is useful for a more detailed account of the changing ideas of "nature" throughout the eighteenth century. The main point is to illustrate how widely acceptable was the notion that "the laws of Nature are the laws of reason."

Index

Addison, Joseph: *Spectator*, 33, 54-55; *Tatler*, 33
Akenside, Mark, 17, 30, 47, 54-56, 57, 97, 114; *Pleasures of Imagination, The*, 54-55, 114-16
Arnold, Matthew: "Dover Beach," 71; "Stanzas from the Grande Chartreuse," 103
Aubin, Robert, 56

Bacon, Francis, 33
Bailey, Margery, 45
Beattie, James, 57
Beautiful, tradition of the, 56, 78-79, 87, 95, 100, 103, 107-108, 110-11, 112-13, 153
Beddoes, Thomas Lovell, 121
Bentham, Jeremy: *Introduction to Principles of Morals and Legislation*, 25
Berkeley, George, 114
Blair, Robert, 130; "The Grave," 129
Blake, William, 128, 144, 147, 149, 153; *Four Zoas, The*, 151; *Songs of Experience*, 66; "Vision of the Last Judgment, A," 151
Bloom, Harold, 78, 142
Bloomfield, Nathaniel, 46, 47
Bloomfield, Robert, 18, 47; *Farmer's Boy, The*, 30, 46
Boileau, 47
Boswell, James: *Life of Johnson*, 35
Bowles, William Lisle, 48, 49, 65
Bronson, Bertrand, 75, 112
Browne, Thomas: *Religio Medici*, 22
Burke, Edmund, 55, 78, 114; *Sublime and the Beautiful, The*, 30, 79, 116, 133
Burton, Robert: *Anatomy of Melancholy*, 35

Butler, Joseph: *Analogy of Religion*, 23
Byron, Lord, 15, 21, 153

Cassirer, Ernst, 38
Coldham and Enfield, 15, 16, 19, 20
Coleridge, Samuel Taylor, 24, 32, 48, 49, 74, 89, 92, 153; "Dejection: An Ode," 88; "Religious Musings," 141-43; *Rime of the Ancient Mariner*, 93
Collins, William, 41, 56, 71, 73, 75, 79, 96-97, 153; "Ode on the Poetical Character," 75; "Ode to Evening," 97, 98; "Ode to Fear," 109; "Ode to Pity," 97; "Ode to Simplicity," 77-78; "Passions, The," 78, 92, 111, 112-13
Cowley, Abraham, 33
Cowper, William 56, 75
Crabbe, George, 63

Dante, 72, 73, 74, 155, 156
Deism, 22, 23
Derby, Countess of, 18
Devonshire, Duchess of, 18
Donne, John, 48
Dryden, John, 17, 97, 112; "Alexander's Feast," 96, 111; "Song of St. Cecilia's Day," 96, 111

Fletcher, Giles: *Christ's Victorie and Triumph*, 156
Fuseli, Henry, 72, 74

Gibbon, Edward, 23
Gilpin, William, 55
Godwin, William: *Political Justice*, 25
Goethe, 156
Goldsmith, Oliver, 33-34, 63; *Citizen*

of the World, 34; *Essays,* 17, 33; "Traveler, The," 64
Goldstein, Lawrence, 116, 129
Gray, Thomas, 17, 73, 75, 97, 130, 146; "Elegy Written in a Country Churchyard," 40, 108, 109, 119, 129, 131

Handel, 111
Hartley, David, 114
Hartman, Geoffrey, 78
Hayes, William, 111
Hayley, William, 47
Hervey, James: *Meditations Among the Tombs,* 130
Hill, Thomas, 18
Homer: *Iliad,* 157; *Odyssey,* 126
Hopkins, Gerard Manley, 138
Horace, 17, 97
Hume, David, 55; "On Miracles," 23
Hunt, Leigh, 49

Johnson, Samuel, 35, 63; *Idler,* 33; *Lives of the Poets,* 17, 30; *Rambler,* 33, 34; *Rasselas,* 32, 35, 40
Jones, William Powell, 140

Keats, John, 49, 74, 78, 96, 109, 144, 153; "Ode on a Grecian Urn," 96; "Ode on Melancholy," 66; "Ode to a Nightingale," 113; "On Sitting Down to Read *King Lear* Again," 87
Knight, Richard Payne, 55

Langer, Susanne, 110
Locke, John: *Reasonableness of Christianity,* 22, 114
Lofft, Capel, 18, 71; *Eudosia,* 140

Maclean, Norman, 96, 97
Malthus, Thomas: *Principles of Population,* 25
Milton, John, 17, 31, 56, 96, 99, 144-45; "At a Solemn Music," 111, 113; "Il Penseroso," 30, 35-36, 98, 132; "L'Allegro," 30, 79, 98, 132; "Lycidas," 88, 103, 108, 109, 142; "Ode on the Morning of Christ's Nativity," 142; *Paradise Lost,* 142, 152, 154, 155; *Paradise Regained,* 153, 155-56; *Samson Agonistes,* 59-60
Montaigne, 42
Moore, Thomas, 28
Morris, David B., 50, 145, 150

Napoleon, 25
Nicholson, Marjorie Hope, 148

Ode, the form and tradition, 96-97, 100
"Ossian" (James Macpherson), 57, 126

Paine, Thomas: *Age of Reason,* 23, 25; *Rights of Man,* 25
Paley, William: *Evidences of Christianity,* 23; *Natural Theology,* 24
Parnell, Thomas, 119, 130; "Night-Piece on Death," 129
Picturesque, tradition of the, 55, 56, 57, 58, 63, 64, 66, 68, 73, 107, 110-11, 118, 153
Plutarch, 17
Pope, Alexander, 17, 30, 31, 114
Price, Martin, 134, 152
Price, Sir Uvedale, 55

Rogers, Samuel: *Pleasures of Memory, The,* 36

Scott, Thomas: *Force of Truth,* 18
Shakespeare, William: *Julius Caesar,* 35
Shaftesbury, 3rd Earl of, 38; *Characteristics,* 55
Shelley, Percy Bysshe, 24, 50, 102, 109, 144, 153
Sickels, Eleanor M., 55, 64, 118, 146
Sidney, Philip, 48
Smith, Adam: *Wealth of Nations,* 17
Sonnet, form and tradition, 44-45, 64-72
Southey, Robert, 15, 16, 19, 22, 25, 32, 44, 46, 47, 48-49, 120, 121, 153; *Thalaba the Destroyer,* 48, 49
Spacks, Patricia Meyer, 56, 70, 75

Index

Spenser, Edmund, 48, 153; *Faerie Queene*, 152, 156
Steele, Richard: *Spectator*, 33; *Tatler*, 33
Stephen, Leslie, 22, 23
Sublime, tradition of the, 55, 56, 72, 107, 110, 111, 113, 114-18, 125-26, 131, 133-34, 137, 139-42, 145-46, 148, 150, 153

Tennyson, Lord Alfred: "Tears, Idle Tears," 66
Thomson, James, 17, 30, 65, 70, 71, 118, 125, 155; *Castle of Indolence, The*, 36, 90; "Winter," from *The Seasons*, 117
Tindal, Matthew: *Christianity as Old as the Creation*, 22-23
Tuveson, Ernest, 149

Virgil, 64, 101, 102

Walpole, Horace, 23
Ward, Ned: *London Spy*, 33
Warton, Joseph, 82-83, 96; "Enthusiast, The," 64, 77; "Ode to Fancy," 97, 98, 99; "Ode to Solitude," 97
Warton, Thomas, The Younger, 18, 30, 31, 37, 41, 71, 73, 116, 119, 153; "Pleasures of Melancholy, The," 36, 63-64, 114-15, 133
Wasserman, Earl, 71, 78
Weiskel, Thomas, 78, 110
Whelan, Sister M. Kevin, 41
White, Henry Kirke; earliest poem, 16; early letters, style of, 16, 20; education, 24-25, 26-28; enlightened service as an ideal, 52, 138-39, 144, 150-51; imagery in his writing, 39, 44, 47, 50, 56, 63, 64, 73, 75, 84, 89, 94, 97, 110, 115, 120, 128-29; intellectual confusion, 20, 28-29, 43-44, 138, 153; melancholy, importance of, 31, 35-37

WORKS, POETRY:
"A Hymn for Family Worship," 85; "Ah, who can say," 64-65; "Athanatos," 132-33; "Awake, sweet harp of Judah," 85; "Be hushed, be hushed, ye bitter winds," 95; "By a Female Lunatic to a Lady," 66, 67-68; "Childhood," 135-37; *Christiad, The*, 142, 152-58; "Christmas Day, 1804," 141, 142, 143-44; *Clifton Grove, a Sketch in Verse, with Other Poems*, 18; "Clifton Grove," 56-64, 84; "Commencement of a Poem on Despair," 95-96; "Elegy Occasioned by the Death of Mr. Gill," 108-109; "Eve of Death, The," 96; "Fanny! Upon Thy Breast," 66, 67; "Fragment of an Eccentric Drama," 120-26; "Fragment of an Ode to the Moon," 103; "Genius," 97, 100, 103-105; "Gondoline," 91-95, 96; "Hushed is the lyre," 87-88; "If far from me," 139; "I'm Pleased, and Yet I'm Sad," 66, 68-69; "Lines Supposed to Be Spoken By a Lover," 126-27; "Lines Written in Wilford Churchyard," 129-31; "Lines Written on a Survey of the Heavens," 133, 140-41; "Loud rage the winds without," 117-18; "Music," 110-13; "My Study," 137-38; "Nelsoni Mors," 108; "O give me music," 83, 87; "Ode to H. Fuseli," 72-76; "Oh! thou most fatal of Pandora's train," 119-20; "On Being Confined to School," 16; "On Disappointment," 107-108; "On My Own Character," 22; "On Reading the Poems of Warton," 82-83; "On the Death of Dermody the Poet," 108, 109-10; "On Whit-Monday," 101-102; "Once more, and yet once more," 88-89; "Quick o'er the wintry waste," 140; "Recantatory," 71-72; "Ship-

wrecked Solitary's Song to the Night, The," 84, 85; "Solitude," 66, 69, 84; "Sweet to the gay of heart," 139-40; "Thanatos," 132; "Time," 142, 146-52; "To a Taper," 66, 69-70, 84; "To April," 66, 70-71; "To Contemplation," 97-100, 134-35; "To Midnight," 84, 89; "To My Lyre," 85-87, 97; "To the Earl of Carlisle, K.G.," 105-107; "To the Harvest Moon," 100-101; "To the Herb Rosemary," 81-82; "To the Moon," 65-66; "To the Morning," 102-103; "To the Wind, at Midnight," 89-90; "Unhappy Poet Dermody in a Storm, The," 66, 67; "Wandering Boy, The," 66-67; "Western gale, The," 90-91; "When high romance," 87; "When pride and envy," 80-81; "Written in the Prospect of Death," 127-29; "Ye Unseen Spirits," 66, 70; "Yes, my stray steps have wandered," 138-39; "Yes, once more that dying strain," 88, 89

WORKS, PROSE:
Lecture on "Genius," 17; *Melancholy Hours,* 18, 23-24, 27, 31, 32, 34, 36-53, 71, 120

White, John, 15, 16, 21
White, Mary, 15
White, Neville, 15, 16, 18, 21
Wordsworth, William, 32, 37, 48, 50, 60-61, 63, 80, 89, 90, 92, 114, 130, 143, 144, 147, 153; *Descriptive Sketches,* 57-58; "Evening Walk, An," 57; "Intimations of Immortality," 96; *Lyrical Ballads, The,* 38, 75, 153; "Ode to Duty," 96; "Resolution and Independence," 88, 144; "Tintern Abbey," 37, 58, 70, 99, 131

Young, Edward, 17, 45, 119, 153; *Night Thoughts,* 127, 145-48, 150-52